The Inclusion Marathon

The Inclusion Marathon

On Diversity and Equity in the Dutch Workplace
(an extensive summary)

Kauthar Bouchallikht
Zoë Papaikonomou

English Translation:
Elodie Kona

Amsterdam University Press

A translated summary of: *De inclusiemarathon: Over diversiteit en gelijkwaardigheid op de werkvloer.* Amsterdam University Press 2021

© Kauthar Bouchallikht & Zoë Papaikonomou / Amsterdam University Press 2021

Translation: Elodie Kona

Cover illustration: Merel Corduwener
Author's photo: Tengbeh Kamara

Cover design: Coördesign, Leiden
Lay-out: Crius Group, Hulshout

ISBN   978 90 4855 839 1
e-ISBN   978 90 4855 840 7 (ePub)
NUR   740

© K. Bouchallikht & Z. Papaikonomou / Amsterdam University Press B.V.,
Amsterdam 2023

Printed and bound by CPI Group (UK) Ltd, Croydon, CR0 4YY

Table of Contents

Preface

The workplace of today is an extraordinarily complex institution. Since the birth of management theory, organizational science has had to evolve with the demands of labor movements, the cultural needs of expanding into new global markets and the changing demographics of the workforce. However, it failed to reflect how all of these shifts are connected. The Diversity, Equity and Inclusion (DEI) industry, born initially out of the U.S. civil rights movement, grew to account for these changes little by little over time. But in its current state, it can feel daunting, overwhelming, and even disjointed for those looking to enter the field or shift to doing DEI work within their organizations.

And although *The Inclusion Marathon* was written for the Netherlands, its lessons, insights and tools are applicable around the world. The authors have contextualized DEI as both a workplace necessity and catalyst for societal change, through an understanding of both the legacy of Dutch colonial and imperial history and its often-esoteric present-day effects. It is a book that should be in the library of anyone who is interested in not just DEI, but organizational dynamics and social change.

At a time when we're all struggling to make sense of all of these growing complexities, the authors maximize the use of the greatest tool that has yet to be leveraged fully in DEI work: the power of the collective. Kauthar and Zoë meticulously interviewed 41 practitioners and researchers to get their views, insights and methods for effective DEI work and, with dedication and intention, included the most powerful and groundbreaking insights in their book. The care that the authors took in including thoughts and concepts that may push readers outside of their comfort zone is a virtual masterclass in objective and collective writing.

Those of us working, living and breathing DEI know in our bones that we are interconnected—as humans, as practitioners, as learners and as nations. We are influenced and impacted by each other in a million little (and big) ways. So, as you go through this book, you'll also find a million little and big ways in which the concepts, practices and harms created by a lack of a DEI lens are mirrored in many cultures. The *look and feel* of the microaggressions, inequity and injustice might differ, for example, but they are still there. The book might speak of the Dutch constitution, but companies not applying the constitution in practice – and even the fact that the constitution was written when only a certain group held power – those truths go beyond the Netherlands. DEI work is exceptionally complex because every organization and nation has their own cultures and contexts, so a multinational likely cannot apply the same *exact* approaches to DEI in their offices in Singapore as they do in Germany, for example. What Kauthar and Zoë have done, however, is take that complexity and create a dynamic start-build-sustain format that can be applied across cultures and contexts.

This extensive summary of the Inclusion Marathon is a must-read for all who are interested in understanding the differences and similarities that countries around the world, like the Netherlands, are grappling with to understand and deconstruct their own identity-based power dynamics. It is a brave interrogation of Dutch image of self–a bold and necessary step in the quest for a better future. They give us real, evidence-based hope that change on a global scale is possible and that the currents of oppression are shifting, so long as we continue the real work and not succumb to the self-serving temptations of profit-driven, performative DEI.

Shiva Roofeh & Farzin Farzad
DEI experts focused on organizational justice

Introduction

It was a cold March morning in 2020. The coronavirus was beginning to tighten its grip on the Netherlands. Our government was urging people to stop shaking hands, to wash their hands thoroughly and to cough and sneeze into their elbows. We met at Amsterdam's Lloyd Hotel half an hour before our first interview appointment for our research on *The World of the Diversity Practitioner*, which was what we were calling this book at the time. For this first interview, we had arranged to meet two seasoned trainers and experts in the field of diversity, equity and inclusion (DEI): Ismahan Çürük and Marten Bos.

For two hours, we talked about the exceptional and complex work of diversity practitioners – experts who deal with diversity, equity and inclusion in the workplace. Their work is remarkable because it requires personal connections and encounters, sharing deeply felt stories that contain pain but also wisdom. The result of this deep dive may be more significant for the workers who are more likely to be excluded due to historical inequality and prevailing norms. The complexities of the diversity practitioners' task lie in the reasons and mechanisms underlying that exclusion.

Working toward more diverse and inclusive organizations is not always cozy and cuddly. Diversity practitioners challenge the status quo and seek to change entrenched norms, ideas, structures and practices. They expose power relationships and privilege. They operate within organizations' areas of exclusion and discrimination. They are the signal-jammers, the killjoys who pour salt on every metaphorical slug of inequality and filter out the noise to keep things on point.[1]

Our conversation with Ismahan Çürük and Marten Bos was an excellent start to our collective journey. Over the following year, we interviewed 41 diversity practitioners and researchers in the Netherlands about the ever-expanding field of diversity and inclusion.

From a global pandemic to Black Lives Matter

Six days after our first interview, the Netherlands went into lockdown. Schools, stores, sports clubs – everything shut down. People worked from home if they could. Healthcare professionals worked overtime to provide the best possible care for COVID patients. Within a few weeks, it dawned on people: we are living through a pandemic. And that pandemic exposed inequality in many areas of our society, including in the workplace.

The COVID-19 pandemic has had significant economic consequences. In times of economic downturn, working on diversity and inclusion usually fades into the background.[2] The benefits of DEI are not recognized, and many companies see it as a "luxury issue", as noted by Halleh Ghorashi, Professor of Diversity and Integration at VU University Amsterdam. However, working on diversity, equity and inclusion sporadically or suddenly stopping DEI projects is disastrous, especially during such a sensitive change process. American diversity practitioner and journalist Janice Gassam Asare compares this situation to training a muscle; if you stop training, the muscle gets weaker. It's important to stay active.[3]

In the United States, the inequality exposed by the pandemic has fueled outrage and energized the struggle around the centuries of disadvantage some groups have suffered. The virus and its fallout have hit Americans in lower socioeconomic positions the hardest, especially Black Americans and Americans from immigrant backgrounds. Working on diversity, equity and inclusion during this crisis has become even more critical because those who experience exclusion in the workplace have been affected the most.[4]

In late May of 2020, protests broke out in the United States that spread across the globe. The catalyst was the murder of Black American George Floyd by a white police officer, who held his knee on Floyd's neck during an arrest. The long history of police brutality against Black Americans and the societal consequences of the corona pandemic initiated a massive expansion of and support for the Black Lives Matter movement. This movement emerged in the summer of 2013 following the acquittal of neighborhood watchman George Zimmerman for the murder of a Black teenager, Trayvon Martin. Three Black American women founded the *#BlackLivesMatter* movement: Alicia Garza, Patrisse Cullors and Opal Tometi.[5]

In an interview with a Dutch online platform *Nieuw Wij* – which reports on diversity, equity and inclusion – Aminata Cairo, a scholar and consultant on inclusion and leadership who lived in the USA for decades, described the importance of the BLM movement:

> Black people's stories opened up the conversation for all of us, as the injustice is so apparent. What does this mean for our self-image? What does that mean for who we aspire to be? [...] We share the pain now, but that also amplifies the pain. But at the same time, the resistance to change is also growing. It shakes us to the core, but that's likely necessary. We need these kinds of movements to create change. It hurts. And pain is not logical. We often want to react to pain very calmly and pleasantly, but that's impossible. People scream, shout and topple statues. If everything were faultless, these reactions wouldn't happen.[6]

The protests also spread to the Netherlands, where thousands of people took to the streets. Several generations of Dutch people would no longer accept discrimination based on skin color and origin, and they loudly demanded change. In the public debate, terms like racism and institutional racism became more frequently used. This crucial social development also affected the diversity practitioners' jobs. Increasing diversity and inclusion in organizations is closely tied to the dynamics of society. (Historical) inequality and stigmatized differences play a significant role in, for example, internship discrimination, entry to and opportunities within the labor market, or feeling safe in the workplace.

The Black Lives Matter movement made many organizations realize the importance of diverse and inclusive workplaces. Organizations soon saw diversity issues as urgent, rather than a luxury to only start thinking about when they had spare time and money. Contrary to what often happens in times of crisis, the economic crisis resulting from the corona crisis hasn't caused a decline in interest in diversity, equity and inclusion. Our interviewees have stayed pretty busy. The awareness they have often had to put effort into creating is developing faster because of the Black Lives Matter movement. Still, there is a big step between an organization realizing that DEI is essential and an organization actually being more inclusive – as we will describe in detail in this extensive summary of *The Inclusion Marathon*.

Our interviews took place online from mid-March 2020 onward. We were Zooming, Skyping and Google-meeting our way through the pandemic. In the Netherlands and around the globe, our interviews were lovingly disrupted by partners, roommates, children or pets. The conversations were reflective, revealing and constructive. In this field, self-knowledge and self-reflection are the starting point of initiated change. Naturally, the professionals who guide these changes excel at this.

We also noticed that our interviewees have a great need to share their experiences and knowledge. The field of diversity and inclusion is young, and diversity practitioners work hard, which can quickly make them feel lonely. They also do the dirty work within organizations: in every nook and cranny, they look for abuse of power, discrimination and exclusion – not the nicest human behaviors. Questioning the status quo is complex and exacting. As the approach to diversity issues varies from one setting to another, diversity practitioners sometimes have little guidance.

That is the main reason why we wrote this book. The knowledge and experiences of Dutch diversity practitioners have not been brought together on a large scale before. These experts shed light on the dark side of organizations and human behavior in order to find ways to create a work environment where everyone is equal. Assembling their insights could yield valuable information because these professionals are out there, day in and day out. They work in all types of organizations: from banks to insurance companies and from municipalities to the commercial and cultural sectors. What do they encounter? How do they approach their work? How do they sustain their work? And what can organizations, employers and managers learn from their experiences?

Context

The Dutch DEI field has grown considerably in recent years. In addition to the practical work that diversity practitioners perform, researchers are conducting more and more studies within this field. An essential examination of the daily activities of diversity practitioners and one of our inspirations for this book is *On Being Included: Racism and Diversity in Institutional Life* (2012) by British-Australian scholar Sara Ahmed.[7] She describes the experiences of diversity practitioners in British and Australian higher education. We recommend this book to all readers who want to delve deeper into this field.

Aspects of inclusion in the workplace are being researched at all major Dutch universities, colleges and vocational schools. The Netherlands also has more and more research on diversity issues within organizations, including studies on those who guide these issues in practice. Here are just some of the parties and researchers working on these issues in the Netherlands:
- the work of Halleh Ghorashi and her team at VU University Amsterdam on power relations within diversity and inclusion;
- the Dutch Inclusivity Monitor, for which a team from Utrecht University led by Naomi Ellemers is mapping and researching the diversity and inclusion policies of organizations;
- Jojanneke van der Toorn is conducting research at Leiden University on the well-being of LGBTQIA+ employees in the workplace;

- Marieke van den Brink and her colleagues at Radboud University Nijmegen research change, resistance and power within organizations;
- the research of Karen van Oudenhoven-van der Zee and her colleagues at VU University Amsterdam on diversity in management;
- Several universities of applied sciences have professorships in the area of diversity and inclusion, such as the professorship on Diversity at Leiden University of Applied Sciences led by Saniye Çelik and the professorship on Diversity Issues at Inholland University of Applied Sciences led by Machteld de Jong;
- Within the field of vocational education, several institutes are working on diversity and inclusion, such as the institute Valuing Differences led by Birgit Pfeifer; and
- The national knowledge institute *Movisie* and the *Kennisplatform inclusief samenleven* (Knowledge Platform for Inclusive Coexistence) contribute with several practical studies on diversity and inclusion in the workplace.

In addition to research on diversity and inclusion within organizations, many critical studies in the Netherlands and abroad shed light on the darker sides of the DEI field: racism, sexism, ableism, trans hatred, Muslim hatred, homophobia, abuse of power and exclusion. The vital work of Philomena Essed, Gloria Wekker, Nancy Jouwe, Willem Schinkel, Aminata Cairo, Domenica Ghidei Biidu, Sinan Çankaya, Sara Ahmed, Edward Said, Houria Bouteldja, Audre Lorde and others is indispensable to our interviewees. It is impossible to mention all the valuable research contributions in one paragraph. That's why we've included a reading list with recommendations for those who want to delve further into this field. This list in the final pages of our book is not exhaustive, but hopefully, it will be a great start to further exploration.

The research and studies mentioned above play an important role in our book. Still, the knowledge and experience of the diversity practitioners were our focal points. After all, they are the best choice to articulate what is happening within organizations whose goal is to make their workplaces more diverse and inclusive. We are delighted that over thirty diversity practitioners dared to openly share what happens when they enter organizations and start doing their thing. We spoke with people who work on diversity issues internally and as external consultants. They are active within different organizations (from the government to commercial companies). They are well-known in the field for their achievements and represent a growing group of courageous pioneers.

Additionally, we interviewed eight scholars based in the Netherlands, who have been researching the various aspects of diversity and inclusion within organizations for many years. Their insights provide an additional layer to contextualize our interviewees' experiences.

Before we take you through our research, we have a few remarks. We regularly used the significant term equity; it's also mentioned in this book's subtitle. In the first chapter, Definitions, we go into more detail about its meaning and why we want to add this concept to the Netherlands' established set of words: 'diversity and inclusion'.

Our interviewees all experience a common denominator within diversity work: *happy talk* is always lurking. Happy talk is the desire to keep everything relating to diversity light and airy.[8] Well-known statements such as 'diversity uplifts an organization', 'diversity is great' and 'diversity creates creativity' are all true. However, getting those positive results requires hard work and not shying away from discomfort and conflict.[9] Talking about (in)equality brings up the fact that we are all different and come from diverse identities and historical contexts. It involves people being treated differently for unfounded reasons due to power dynamics. That's why it is crucial to constantly be aware of how exclusion occurs in society and the workplace. The concept of 'equity' helps foster this awareness.

Language is vital in the diversity, equity and inclusion (DEI) conversation. Language can include or exclude people. For example, think of people who do not feel comfortable being addressed with the personal pronouns 'she' or 'he' and prefer to use 'they' or 'them'. Language also exposes historical inequalities. This is one of the reasons why we follow the Associated Press guideline to write the word *Black* with a capital letter.[10]

In this book, we use wording that is part of the conversation about diversity, equity and inclusion in the Netherlands at the time of writing (2021).[12] In the selected quotes, we use our interviewee's exact words, even when they do not always match our choice of words.

We tried to do justice to the experiences and knowledge of all interviewees. Ultimately, this book is the result of our analysis. It is, therefore, not a literal representation of the interviewees' opinions on the subject and its different aspects. The same goes for the tone of this book. The tones of our interviewees differ, as do ours. Sometimes, the conversation about diversity, equity and inclusion seems more about style than content. Always emphasizing tone distracts from the content and the message at hand.

"So, diversity is everything?" Professor of Diversity, sociologist and author Lucho Rubio Repáraz sometimes gets this question from colleagues. If you define diversity the way the dictionary does, as a variety of things or variation, then yes. In that case, diversity is the variety in everything, which means diversity is everything. Although we would have liked to display every bit of the diversity practitioner's world – all perspectives, all insights – that is, of course, impossible. With this book, we hope to make a modest contribution to the further professionalization of this field and offer tools to organizations and executives who want to work towards diverse, inclusive and equitable workplaces.

With our journey through the world of the diversity practitioner, we refer, as described earlier, to the many scientific studies published on diversity and inclusion in the workplace. In this book, we also expand on *'Heb je een boze moslim voor mij'?* ('Got an angry Muslim for me?'), a book on inclusive journalism written by this book's coauthor Zoë Papaikonomou with Annebregt Dijkman. We also build upon her research on power and discomfort within diversity and inclusion for the online platform *Nieuw Wij*.[13] As a result, you will frequently find references to these sources in the text and footnotes.

Reading guide

We realized something during the journey through the world of diversity practitioners. The interviewees' knowledge and experience are highly relevant, not only to other diversity practitioners and researchers, but also to organizations, administrators and executives who want to contribute to more diverse, inclusive and equal workplaces. Therefore, we have also chosen to include two chapters written from the organization's and manager's points of view.

In the first chapter – *Definitions* – we explain the terms diversity, equity and inclusion (DEI) by connecting our interviewees' definitions.

The second chapter – *Society* – explores the interaction between organizations and society. How do social developments influence work culture and the DEI field?

In the third chapter – *The Organization* – we reflect on our interviewees' experience and knowledge on how to start the inclusion marathon as an organization and sustain it. This chapter discusses exploring the diversity landscape, setting up diversity policies, shaping recruitment and selection processes, and creating a safe work environment.

In the fourth chapter – *The Manager* – we try to unravel power and leadership using the core idea "With power comes responsibility". Among other things, we discuss self-reflection, vulnerability and dealing with discomfort and conflict.

The fifth chapter – *The Diversity Practitioner* – is entirely devoted to the world of the Dutch diversity practitioner. Who are these diversity experts and how did they get into this field? How do they tackle complex issues? And how do they keep up their work?

The sixth chapter – *Knowledge is Power* – deals with the question: how can science be valuable and connect with the practice of diversity work? Especially when working toward more diverse, inclusive, and equitable workplaces, making this connection is sometimes challenging. Scientific knowledge is also bound by norms and founded partly on historical inequality.

This English extensive summary of *The Inclusion Marathon* is of course less complete than the original book. Nevertheless, we hope that the core of our findings can make a modest contribution to the international DEI field.

At the back of the book, you will find the biographies of all the people we interviewed. For readability's sake, we will not use their complete job titles at every mention. The three (practical) chapters – the organization, the manager and the diversity practitioner – consist of three parts: how to start, how to build and how to sustain. The practical-minded reader might start with these chapters. But let's face it: if you sincerely want to work toward more diverse, inclusive and equitable workplaces, you'll have to start from scratch. Reading this book is not enough; you'll have to start analyzing yourself. It is no coincidence that you'll often encounter the words *self-knowledge* and *self-reflection* in the coming pages. Anyone who wants to take part in a marathon must determine their starting point and be unafraid to face themselves, both at every turn and throughout the entire race. And that won't always be pleasant.

Definitions

What's in a name?

This first chapter defines diversity, equity and inclusion, based on the interviewees' interpretations and by linking their perspectives. As you can imagine, these terms have many definitions. However, our interviewees state that meaningful interpretations arise through joint reflection.

Let's start with a simple definition of these three concepts:
- **diversity** is about differences within a group
- **inclusion** relates to what one does with those differences
- **equity** is about the (power) distinctions within these differences[14]

Popular phrases, such as diversity and inclusion, often become catch-all terms. Unfortunately, they are often used to differentiate individuals or groups from the majority or norm. Moreover, the interpretation of these terms follows societal trends. Inventing new concepts and definitions to keep up with the times is essential, but they can also lead to empty and damaging interpretations. How these terms are interpreted and eventually implemented is a much more vital aspect to consider.

Diversity and inclusion are often used interchangeably, leading to much confusion within organizations and society – and among diversity practitioners and researchers. The commotion surrounding these words may be detrimental to their practical use. Saniye Çelik, a college professor on inclusive leadership, recognizes the risks when these terms are used carelessly: "When mixing up terms like that, inclusion may become a way to disguise the issue at hand." Additionally, these terms are often framed in a certain way to serve a calculated purpose and vested interests. Diversity practitioners plead for open conversations on how these terms are interpreted and how meanings differ by context and individual. Diversity, equity and inclusion (DEI) are defined separately, but we will also discuss how they are intertwined and how diversity practitioners use these meanings in the field. Because DEI stems from processes involving people, organizations and society, it is nearly impossible to encompass its underlying concepts with ready-made definitions.

Diversity is often broadly defined, which leads to a loss of meaning. Hanan Challouki, an expert in inclusive communication, explains: "On the one hand, it's great that we are growing and finding new words because then they might better define what we want to achieve. On the other hand, they must not become meaningless concepts either."

Let's diversify!

Diversity is about *difference*. More specifically, it's about differences relative to a group. Diversity can be visible, such as gender and skin color, or it can be invisible, like character, sexuality and religion. There's a dangerous pitfall: when an individual characteristic is emphasized, one person becomes responsible for conveying the group's diversity and representing a minority. This is also known as tokenism. It's when an organization symbolically puts someone forward from a minority group to make a good impression. Alternatively, this pitfall can be referred to as essentialism, which often manifests as pictures depicting stereotypes and short one-off workshops on diversity without long-lasting and sustainable changes. In these cases, people are often seen as only the characteristics that makes them 'diverse' relative to the dominant group.

Lucho Rubio Repáraz, sociologist and Professor of Diversity at Leiden University of Applied Sciences, explains what diversity means in its essentialist form: "Diversity is more than a definition or a concept; it has become a catch-all term to indicate what's considered outside the norm or dominant group. It actually concerns everyone. In the Netherlands, many people view diversity as 'what isn't part of the norm'. Previously used umbrella terms were 'interculturalism' or 'multiculturalism'. Now, diversity is trending. Yet, this is still a broad and generic concept."

As human beings, we should fully embrace individuals without reducing them to what makes them different from the majority group. People are more than just an embodied symbol or visual representation of a minority group. We mustn't lose sight of the fact that people consist of layers upon layers of identities and sub-identities. Also, identities evolve constantly and are dynamic. People have many identities. In different contexts, different identities are more accentuated than others and how an individual gets approached can differ. "People often pretend that one's identity is fixed, but that is not true. Identity is constantly evolving. It's always in motion," adds Manuela Kalsky, Professor of Theology and Society. It is therefore crucial to keep an eye out for all forms of diversity, visible and invisible, but to remain aware of inequality and exclusion.

Also, there can be 'identity-blind policies'. These policies don't pay specific attention to the characteristics that make employees different from the norm. Inclusivity researcher Onur Şahin says, "Organizations often boast, 'We treat everyone equally'. But the reality is different. It might be well-intentioned to treat everyone equally, but that backfires because some people are more easily discriminated against and are hence treated unequally." As we'll discuss later in this chapter, equality focuses on similarities: everything and everyone is the same. In a society with differences in power and privilege, equity is a better fit. Not everyone's the same or similar, but everyone deserves equal rights, despite these differences. Or better yet, because of those differences.

In a nutshell, broad definitions increase the risk of ironing out pain points and inequalities. Companies should look out for these detrimental effects to prevent an organization from looking diverse on the outside but not the inside. It is also important to remain clear on what definition an organization chooses, as this choice reflects how every level of the organization interprets diversity.

Join the party and dance along! What's inclusion?

Diversity practitioners agree that diversity and inclusion are like breathing in and out. Inclusion does not come after diversity but goes with it, just like breathing. Inclusion is the idea that people get to be themselves, but it also means their input is valued and people listen to them. Everyone is allowed to participate without having to fit into a normative mold. Mary Tupan-Wenno explains briefly: "Inclusion is about keeping people in and not just bringing them in." She is the Executive Director at ECHO, Center of Expertise for Diversity Policy, which advises companies and institutions on diversity and inclusion.

All in all, more diversity does not necessarily lead to more inclusion. Besides, the more divergence within a group of people, the fewer people feel included, because this often leads to tensions. How you deal with that conflict is the key question.

There should be space for differences to exist. Inclusion is about literal and figurative accessibility and how that accessibility is tailored to all workers. Permission to participate goes even further: feeling safe and at home. Creating this inclusiveness is a shared process and should not be tailored to and imposed by the majority. Organizations can move towards an inclusive work environment by keeping the conversation going and not making assumptions. Martin van Engel, Program Manager at the Van Gogh Museum, describes how diversity and inclusion differ, "With diversity, you can check off partial identities. Inclusion is the degree to which someone has the potential to be(come) a full-fledged member of a group." Elsa van de Loo, lawyer and trainer at the Netherlands Institute of Human rights, further illustrates this by using Verna Myers' famous party metaphor, which doesn't go far enough: "Inclusion is not just being allowed to dance along at the party, but also being allowed to decide what music to dance to."

We speak of false inclusion, when not everyone can decide on the playlist. When someone doesn't feel like dancing, this should be made possible as well. Inclusion is not just being allowed to participate but also being able to question how power structures determine what inclusion means. Do you have to conform to the norm and meet imposed conditions? Professor of Gender and Diversity, Marieke van den Brink, observes what happens when inclusion comes with disadvantages. "You can become part of the group, but others impose explicit or implicit conditions for its membership. Take off your facial piercings, wear certain clothes or laugh along with certain jokes. Sometimes, you get to keep your uniqueness, but then you never really become part of a group."

Equity versus Equality

One must become aware of how some people and communities are left out. Equity thus emphasizes the inequality built on historic grounds and power dynamics. Our interviewees refer to equity as an essential condition for an all-encompassing D&I workspace. It emphasizes the space needed for differences and highlights how exclusion and exploitation have come about due to the history of imperialism, colonialism and slavery. So, equity is not the same as equality.

The use of the concept of equity is relatively new in the Dutch DEI context. The Dutch term 'gelijkwaardigheid' is not a one-to-one translation of equity. And that also has consequences for our elaboration of this term. Our elaboration is based on the knowledge and experiences of Dutch diversity practitioners and can therefore differ from the explanation of equity in the international context.

Equality has two meanings in relation to diversity and inclusion. As a legal term, the principle of equality is enshrined in Article 1 of the Dutch Constitution: 'All persons in the Netherlands shall be treated equally in equal circumstances. Discrimination on the grounds of religion, belief, political opinion, race or sex or on any other grounds whatsoever shall not be permitted.' The second definition states that something or someone is the same. This last interpretation has its pitfalls.[15]

Equity is about the fact that something or someone does not have to be the same, but – despite or because of the differences – is worth the same and has equal rights. Thus, equity is a more appropriate term because it includes the uniqueness of people. Not everyone is equal. If you assume otherwise, you shape others in your image. Hence, the pitfall of the term 'equality'.

Our interviewees indicate that equality as a legal term is crucial to their work, but its second meaning is a bit more tricky. When you assume everyone is the same (or equal), you are likely trying to mold another person in your image and assess them based on your ideas and perspectives. Equity is more useful because it values each individual's uniqueness. In an interview with the online platform Nieuw Wij, Philomena Essed, Professor of Critical Race, Gender and Leadership Studies at Antioch University in the United States, describes the importance of equity:

> Many people risk or lose their lives to preserve their self-esteem. They go on hunger strikes or fight oppression and threats because they do not accept living in degrading conditions or having their beliefs violated. We all need to feel worthy of walking this earth. But there is a limit to worthiness, namely when individuals or groups of people start to believe they are worth more than others. The basic concept of dignity or worthiness is that we are equal to each other. People feel their dignity is violated when others insult them or their beliefs. What does it mean when every human life is equally worthy? It is important to start with this question. Not as a cliché or a popular slogan, but as a way of reflecting on the implications of this premise.[16]

It is crucial to keep in mind that diversity and inclusion within organizations occur in the context of a society where structures of exclusion and discrimination also exist; therefore, equity is much more feasible. That's how the so-called *happy diversity discourse* develops, one that only emphasizes what diversity can contribute and not how leaders address organizational power structures. Diversity and inclusion become, as it were, symbols to name problems but not to solve them. Fatima Elatik, an experienced government advisor, describes diversity and inclusion as band-aids we use to cover the rot of our system: "Governments and agencies are dealing with diversity and inclusion as some objective to tick all the boxes, while intrinsically not dealing with what it actually means. It should be about leadership, integrity within institutions, protecting, upholding and respecting human rights, and responsible leaders."

The question remains: to what extent is there space within the organization to be critical of leaders and organizational structures? For example, how safe do employees feel in their daily work lives? Diversity practitioners notice that it is not easy to point out organizations' responsibilities. Sometimes, the professionals themselves are even identified as the problem, especially when they drop the word 'diversity'. That's why they find it so important to choose the right words, tone and timing. Diversity practitioners want to avoid losing support, so they start conversations within organizations at the right time.

While some organizations prefer not to talk about diversity, it remains important. In brief, it is essential to be mindful of all forms of diversity while staying aware of equity. To assume equal treatment for all means not recognizing that some people are treated unequally and marginalized within society. That's why we stress the importance of equity rather than equality. The idea that everyone has the same opportunities is typical of liberal market thinking. Many researchers place this phenomenon under ethnocentrism, in which the other culture is considered inferior, leading to an us-versus-them mentality that perpetuates inequality. Astrid Elburg, a leadership consultant and coach, says: "The same knowledge in another body is worth less. This way of thinking affects every aspect of one's career path."

In that quote, Astrid Elburg means that some differences, and therefore some people, are more valued than others. So, it is crucial to let go of your frames of reference. However, judgmental thinking is deeply ingrained in our society. In the Netherlands, these biases can be traced back to power relationships from the colonial period, in which a person is seen as subordinate to the 'helping' hand. Halleh Ghorashi, Professor of Diversity and Integration, sees this mechanism in the Netherlands and Scandinavian countries in the welfare state context. "Here, diversity and inclusion are equal to 'caring for the weaker groups'." Hence, diversity practitioner Jeftha Pattikawa, reminds people to be aware of societal developments and power dynamics: "You can have a very diverse and inclusive organization but still maintain colonial structures and mentality. Those don't fit our society anymore, so organizations should keep up with these societal shifts."

Inequity also exists in knowledge. It is reflected in language usage, among other things. Think of terms like 'non-Western' and 'Western', where a distinction is made and 'the other' is excluded. Language and how we define words matter. As Inclusive Program Leader at the National Archives, Jeftha Pattikawa knows how history affects knowledge. He explains, "Our profession critically questions white, male, heteronormative and Eurocentric perspectives in organizations. I'm always cautious with the term 'evidence-based', because there's a dynamic even in our field where you see that other forms of knowledge are not given space when it comes to race, gender or class."

Since definitions are important when considering different interpretations, we also discuss Kimberlé Crenshaw's concept of intersectionality: a way of understanding why some groups are excluded and others are not, based on identities such as ethnicity, gender, language, status, you name it. This linguistic approach allows us to remain critical of DEI within organizations and how it relates to society as a whole.

In an interview with the Dutch media platform *Nieuw Wij*, Sarita Bajnath, a coach and trainer on privilege and intersectionality, explains further:

> Intersectionality is a way of understanding how the world works and why some groups are excluded, and others are not.

This understanding gives insight into how certain aspects affect a person, such as education, ethnicity, language, class, orientation, color, status and so on. These facets have an impact on what you experience in life and how you are treated.[17]

American civil rights lawyer Kimberlé Crenshaw coined the term intersectionality. Crenshaw handled a case in which a group of people was being discriminated against within a company. They turned out to be Black women, specifically. Men were not discriminated against, and not all women were discriminated against, just Black women. She could not legally substantiate this at the time, as discrimination was not yet perceived in an intersectional way. Thus, the concept of intersectionality was born.[18]

Society

Society is diverse but not necessarily inclusive. Moreover, people are not always treated equally. Inequality and exclusion affect people in their daily lives and therefore affect their experiences in the workplace. Just think of comments like: "Where are you really from?" Or homophobic and racist jokes disguised as friendly banter. Those affected by these micro-aggressions find it difficult to indicate how and why others should tackle conversations differently. Leadership coach Esther Mollema points out the danger of these prejudices and ways of thinking: "If you can't point out the unconscious biases because the perpetrator feels threatened, then nothing will ever change."

So, when discussing diversity and inclusion, being reflective and self-critical is a prerequisite. You have to dare to step out of your comfort zone. Only then will a constructive conversation arise on a level playing field.

The Constitution Article 1

Article 1 in the Dutch Constitution can be a common starting point for DEI policy. However, organizations often don't sufficiently apply the Constitution in practice. Observing how a company implements the law every day is vital. Rules and regulations on paper are not enough; they must actually be enforced and applied.

There should be an ongoing discussion about how organizations relate to democratic principles and society. Carel Boers, co-founder of *Integere Overheid*, a Dutch platform that connects government officials and professionals to stimulate honest and transparent governance, points to the fact that Article 1 – first drafted in 1798 – is essentially anything but equal. "The law was written when only white men held power and controlled public life. Authorities drew it up in the period of colonial leadership when inhabitants of the colonies fought against inequality, and no news of the oppressed peoples was allowed to reach the Netherlands."

Like minorities in the workplace, diversity practitioners experience resistance when addressing and effectively tackling exclusion and discrimination in the workplace. They are often criticized and personally attacked. Sometimes it even costs them their jobs. It takes courage to bring up DEI, let alone set about making changes within an organization. Saniye Çelik, a diversity lecturer, describes how striving for equality in the workplace can cause the dominant group to feel excluded. "From the moment you are trying to eliminate inequity, a large group stands up and says, 'Now we feel excluded'."

Exclusion

Internal dynamics and work cultures sometimes get in the way of workplace equality because social exclusion is also reflected within organizations. Thus, (work) culture is why Article 1 of the Constitution doesn't always manifest in the workplace. Inclusivity researcher Onur Şahin states: "An organization is part of society; social processes don't suddenly disappear in a workplace environment."

As stated before, putting laws on paper just doesn't cut it. Prejudice and stereotypes can still undermine regulations intended to enforce equity and prevent discrimination. Manuela Kalsky, Professor of Theology and Society, points out the ever-changing relationships in society due to the fight against discrimination and racism: "It is quite possible that if you want to become a professor and are white, the position will go to an equally quali-fied Black woman. I call that a social gain, even if it is a bit tough to handle on a personal level."

Colonialism and the Dutch 'empty tolerance'

History is the foundation of our society and still affects our current ways of thinking. In other words, the colonial past still influences how reality takes shape, how shared history is discussed and where power lies. Gloria Wekker, an expert on colonialism and race, states that a paradox characterizes the Dutch self-image: racism evokes strong emotions while people often deny its very existence.[19]

Jeftha Pattikawa, Inclusion Program Director at the National Archives, says structures in Dutch society from the imperial and colonial past continue to reverberate in people's minds and, thus, in organizations. The critical question when considering historical evolutions is: whose voices are (not) given space in the shared history of human civilization?

The image of the Netherlands as a progressive and tolerant state is unbalanced and does not match reality. Social change is about questioning inequality and the balance of power; otherwise, one gets stuck with 'empty tolerance'. Esther Mollema, an advisor on entrepreneurship and leadership, illustrates: "Ever since the 17th century, we have been admitting people to the Netherlands, but mostly for commercial profit and as cheap labor. The Dutch empty tolerance: 'at least we have something to gain from these imported immigrants. They may stay here, as long as they don't make anyone's life difficult. And don't take me out of my comfort zone'."

"Out of the comfort zone, that's where the magic happens." But when it comes to social change, resistance usually comes up and stepping out of the comfort zone seems like a step too far. To sum up, if power dynamics and unequal structures do not change, there is no space for constructive conversations and 'empty tolerance' ensues.

Movements

Several movements have emerged to bring about change in response to societal injustices (i.e., discrimination, hate campaigns, racism, polarization, exclusion, etc.). There is undoubtedly an interaction between societal movements like #MeToo, Black Lives Matter and similarly oriented organizations. In the Netherlands, there is a movement known as Kick Out Zwarte Piet (KOZP).[20] This action group seeks to abolish the racist portrayal of Black Pete (Zwarte Piet). Also, social initiatives are being set up to work together, battling their shared struggles against inequality.

Esther Mollema explains how awareness of these discrepancies can elicit shame about where society stands and the way that painful and uncomfortable confrontations can be the catalyst for change: "Individuals are touched when confronted with these struggles, which makes it possible to develop a sharper DEI policy. You have to become radically inclusive and ensure that no more people are against inclusion within your organization. I'm a big believer in equality by design, which means looking your systems over and wondering: Are they fair to everyone?"

The world in the workplace

Martin Luther King, Jr. once said: "Injustice anywhere is a threat to justice everywhere." International developments impact the Netherlands and vice versa. Some examples are Black Lives Matter and the Pride Movement. Also, societal actions affect the workplace, such as #MeToo. Thus, developments in society confirm the urgency of specific issues; professionals within organizations need less justification as to why diversity, equity and inclusion are necessary.

Systems of exclusion and oppression are repeated and re-inforced globally. That much is clear. However, it also works the other way around: movements that oppose exclusion and oppression have had a global effect. National Archives Program Manager Jeftha Pattikawa sees how developments surrounding different forms of injustice are spreading worldwide and how they are all intertwined: "Societies are straightening out asymmetrical relations between the genders and social classes, for instance.

An awful lot is happening in societies, and like so, organizations will have to keep up."

Organizations will have to evolve along with society to stay relevant. However, they should address DEI to benefit society and, where necessary, change society, not just to boost their image, out of opportunism, or to make money. Diversity practitioners mention that many companies want to put in place DEI but, at the same time, refuse to be self-critical or are not willing to change where needed.

Diversity as a business model

The extent to which diversity, equity and inclusion are valued as essential depends on economic developments. DEI in the workplace definitely hinges on means and money. Professor Marieke van den Brink studies how organizations relate to social developments such as the Black Lives Matter movement. When organizations support these movements, they may do so for a variety of reasons. The question is to what extent they reflect the movement's call for equality in their organizational processes. "I am a little skeptical about this because you could say that they are showing commitment within the capitalist system to make a good impression. Whether it will actually encourage the organization to look at their organizational processes, and whether they will actually tackle racism on the work floor, remains to be seen."

Unfortunately, diversity, equity and inclusion are often seen as luxury issues; time and money are only devoted to them in times of prosperity. However, the Black Lives Matter movement, among others, has helped DEI become increasingly seen as an urgent issue that always needs attention – especially in times of crisis. This is historically quite exceptional, as diversity, equity and inclusion have often become lower priorities within organizations during times of economic problems.

So, to what extent do organizations implement equity within their organizational processes and structures? There are several motives for corporate social responsibility. If you want to contribute to DEI it is important that you do not see marginalized communities as customers alone, it's even more important to engage these communities and give back to them. According to Hanan Challouki, an expert on inclusive communication, this means: treating your staff equally in the workplace; fair employment practices; investing in talent; and investing in organizations that are committed to DEI. "It's not just about profiting off of diversity, but that you are also giving back to that super-diverse society."

If companies are primarily concerned with profit and a positive image, inequality and exclusion may be reduced to marketing. Manuela Kalsky believes money is only part of a more significant equation to success within organizations: "A company wants to make a profit; that is understandable. Research shows that companies with diversified teams achieve better results and are more successful. But what about your corporate culture? How much room is there for diversity? You can assess subjective aspects with objective measures, such as the drop-out rate, the increase in burnouts or young people leaving the company immediately after their training. All of this costs the company money, so it should be calculated and translated into a concrete figure."

The extent to which diversity, equity and inclusion are recognized as crucial is also influenced by economic developments. In times of economic downturn, diversity, equity and inclusion are considered lower priorities. Professor Halleh Ghorashi says this way of approaching diversity issues can seem like fashion trends: "When the economy is struggling, organizations tend to ignore diversity and inclusion. That says something about how we as a society look at these issues. We see them as a pastime, as something that can only be significant in times of prosperity. The Black Lives Matter movement has made many people and organizations realize that diversity and inclusion are not 'luxury issues' but urgent matters. And if you're serious about it as an organization, you must persevere, especially in times of crisis. The corona crisis is the only crisis so far in which diversity and inclusion have remained on the agenda and this is good news."

The Diversity Industry

Halleh Ghorashi describes how "making a profit" has become part of diversity work. The idea of the business case for diversity within organizations originated in the 1980s in the United States as a reaction to the civil rights movement, which was considered too threatening by the dominant group with terms like 'affirmative action', 'emancipation' and 'power abuse'. However, employers did realize that they needed to attract talent to survive and in the US, with its super-diverse population, that meant being an attractive employer. They started with the question: how do you make sure you're bringing in talent? And later, they added the following question: how do you keep this talent in the organization? The terms 'diversity' and, later on, 'inclusion' came into use and were seen as less threatening because they rarely questioned power relations and inequity.

In European welfare states such as the Netherlands and the Scandinavian countries, diversity and inclusion have different connotations: helping the so-called 'weaker populations' to become 'just like us'. "Diversity and inclusion became a moral imperative. It was no longer about individual talent but about the inclusion of the weaker person. That's not equity but equality, in which everyone becomes 'the same' and differences are ignored," Halleh Ghorashi, Professor of Diversity and Integration clarifies.

Farzin Farzad, an American DEI expert focused on power relations, stresses the importance of remaining critical, mainly to prevent DEI from being (unwittingly) used to perpetuate inequality. He warns against the so-called 'diversity industry', in which policies and interventions are packaged as attractively as possible to sell to organizations. But what use are these new policies if they do not lead to changes within the organization and beyond? "Nowadays, the story of diversity and inclusion keeps revolving around the individual, but nothing changes within the system. Diversity practitioners are inevitably also involved in and (partly) responsible for this development. For instance, people from underrepresented groups are brought in based on

35

'inclusion' and are told to 'be themselves'. But they are still not allowed to challenge the powers that be."

Marieke Van den Brink, Professor of Gender and Diversity, refers to the rise of *accidental activists* who are only driven by economic incentives. "Some recruitment agencies do not necessarily know how gender inequality works but they try to supply to the demand of women for top positions anyhow. It's a neoliberal strategy to make money, but it doesn't address the source of gender inequality in organizations." Nevertheless, it is difficult to spot those with ulterior motives, even for diversity practitioners. So, they should be critical when accepting projects. Even then, an organization can use their advice or training as a temporary band-aid instead of accomplishing viable changes.

Also, some organizations may appear from the outside to be working on diversity, equity and inclusion but actually are not. In so doing, they perpetuate systems of exclusion and oppression, the very things that new social developments are trying to resist. Farzin Farzad emphasizes the question that both organizations and diversity practitioners have to ask themselves: "am I contributing to this problematic system, or am I helping to dismantle it?"

To summarize, as an employer, you have an essential role and responsibility within your organization and society. Our interviewees mentioned three key points to exercising sustainable corporate social responsibility. First, understand and acknowledge inequity in society and power positions; then, offer employees knowledge and experiences to understand these historical and social developments; and, finally, give back to society.

The Organization

In this chapter, diversity practitioners share their insights on how to get started on the inclusion marathon. We interviewed professionals from a variety of organizations, both big and small, who shared examples and discussed many approaches. To take you through the organizational changes, we've divided this chapter into three parts: how to start, how to build and how to sustain. However, these steps do coincide.

HOW TO START

As when running an actual marathon, one must come prepared and have had intense mental and physical preparation before starting on DEI policy and inciting organizational change. The starting point is expanding one's knowledge of the diversity landscape and understanding how to incorporate organizational changes.

Unravel the diversity landscape

DEI is a discipline like any other; it requires expertise and experience to get the most effective and sustainable results. Improving one's knowledge is the ideal starting point. Below we have listed six steps to effectively start the change process within your organization:

Step 1   Recognize the DEI field in its own right. Companies often perceive diversity, equity and inclusion as a nonessential discipline that isn't an essential part of organizational goals.

Step 2   Embrace DEI as a change issue that takes time. As ECHO Executive Director Mary Tupan-Wenno puts it, "Directors need to realize that they are not fighting against the symptoms but for what they want to bring about within their organizations. Investing in diversity, equity and inclusion is not just a one-time thing."

Step 3 When entering the DEI field, it's essential to prepare for the process and formulate the right questions for your organization. Diversity practitioners advise taking a critical step back and coming well-prepared for the process that's about to take place. Senior Advisor on Diversity and Inclusion at the Ministry of Social Affairs and Employment, Shervin Nekuee, says: "I would recommend making an overview of the diversity landscape and the debates that are going on within a company. Recently, I spoke to a CEO who took the time to immerse himself in our field. He sought advice from several experts to prepare himself for the steps ahead. I think that's an excellent start. You first have to slow down and think, in order to speed up later on."

If it were up to Professor of Diversity Halleh Ghorashi, the step of orientation and preliminary research would also involve taking the time to empathize with the stories surrounding DEI. What are the stories surrounding inequality within the organization? Halleh Ghorashi believes experiences should become tangible to allow for a broader connection between people: "It's about striving for openness by allowing diversity, broadening your horizons and enriching them. Only then you can make connections with others in society."

Step 4 Have the courage to allow discomfort and know that mistakes are part of the process. Meanwhile, it's important to remain transparent about your process. All efforts toward change will be put under a magnifying glass, most likely accentuating slip-ups. Diversity practitioners remind us to get ready for some aggressive and uncomfortable revelations. When working on DEI, the vital thing to keep in mind is this: we all make mistakes, but how we deal

	with them and how we remain transparent while going through the change process define your organization's willingness to move toward a more inclusive environment.
Step 5	Dare to look in the mirror. Self-reflection is essential. In other words, you must be open to being corrected and dare to correct yourself. But it would be best if you also learned to evolve with new perspectives. This is not the same as having 'goodwill'. As Halleh Ghorashi puts it: "Goodwill will not get you any further because it always involves a hierarchical relationship; the other person must become like you. Becoming more inclusive is about moving with people, allowing others to be themselves."
Step 6	Invest time and money, because creating awareness requires these resources. Not wanting to invest the time to become more diverse and inclusive is a significant barrier for many organizations. Elsa van de Loo, lawyer and policy advisor, confirms: "If you refuse to make time for training courses or a thorough approach to your recruitment and selection procedure, if everything has to be gone through quickly, then there is no point."

Tips to reduce or eliminate resistance

Diversity practitioners – everyone, really – should increase their awareness about the importance of DEI to curb resistance. "It's like *The Matrix* with a touch of *Alice in Wonderland*. Like taking the red or the blue pill and going down the rabbit hole. Once you've seen it, you can't unsee it," Siela Ardjosemito-Jethoe, Policy Advisor on Diversity and Inclusion, describes.

Awareness is a starting point for an organization to become more diverse and equal. Mohan Verstegen, a physician in the Defense Department and responsible for his unit's diversity policy, puts it this way: "If the need for diversity and inclusion is not explained properly, it leads to resistance." Hanan Challouki, expert on inclusive communication, agrees and states that companies should define what diversity and inclusion mean: "If you can open up that conversation – not just at the management level – but at all levels, then you can think about the steps that need to be taken to communicate about D&I."[21]

By involving all organizational levels and connecting the importance of DEI to daily operations, diversity practitioners create more support for the DEI policies. Joy Lodarmasse, Manager of Diversity and Inclusion at energy network company Alliander, tries to help managers and employees in different parts of the company answer why DEI is so important in their daily work. "The question is: Why would diversity be relevant to you? This differs per department and often per person."

Opposition to diversity, equity and inclusion stems from a feeling of not being heard or seen. Connecting stories and developing a third eye and ear for hidden talent can reduce resistance to change. Diversity practitioner Marten Bos explains the main reason for resistance and fear of change: "People don't want to lose their privilege. They have nothing against diversity as long as nothing changes for them."

Boosting morale with quick wins seems like the way to remove some resistance from 'diversity fatigue'. Diversity fatigue often arises among employees who have been working for a long time to create a more diverse workplace and become discouraged when they see no change or with employees belonging to the norm who do not recognize themselves in the diversity policy and think it is not about them. Quick wins are not a sustainable way to work on DEI and can never stand alone, but they can help enthuse diversity-weary employees. Taking concrete action can also show employees who have been arguing for change that something is happening. Bouchra Talidi, owner of Inclusioncy, adds: "You can sometimes stay in the research phase for too long, but you can also go into action mode too much, while you don't yet know how and why. I try to combine both approaches."

Organizations can reduce or even counteract resistance by focusing on the drivers of diversity, equity and inclusion. Still, some employees will not want to go along. Esther Mollema, an expert in inclusive leadership, emphasizes that it is essential to not give the most attention to these opponents of inclusion but rather to focus on the supporters of DEI and thus get the middle group, those doubting DEI, on board. You get more people involved than you first thought, and you increase the chance of getting skeptics on board: "I always say: the train goes on. Eventually, many people jump on the train while it moves and only a few are left behind."

Hierarchy: where will DEI be housed?

We discussed the best place for a diversity practitioner – or a DEI department – within an organization with our interviewees. First of all, diversity does not belong under the HR department, where members assess how much 'diversity' is present in the workforce. Moreover, a diversity department should have an independent role in challenging the status quo at all levels of the organization. Shervin Nekuee explains why diversity under HR is anything but optimal: "For diversity and inclusion work within an organization, there has to be a strong connection with people and processes in the workplace. HR professionals often only get signals when employees and managers aren't doing their jobs well. At that point, it's often too late to change things for the better." Terence Guiamo, Global Director of Inclusion, Diversity & Belonging at Just Eat Takeaway, also points out that organizations should position a diversity department close to the board of directors and the CEO. "Diversity and inclusion is not an HR topic; it's a business topic, so it has to be within the CEO's reach." According to our interviewees, a diversity department should be linked to all layers in an organization, including the top.

Top management must be the driver of diversity policy; every interviewee indicated this, without exception. However, there must also be a bottom-up approach to get the whole organization on board while ensuring that the top becomes or remains more involved. "If you don't get management on board, then it's a losing battle," National Archives Program Director Jeftha Pattikawa stresses.

HOW TO BUILD

There is no single blueprint for a successful diversity policy because it is context-specific. Each organization operates from different values and experiences different challenges. This section lists some guidelines for building diversity policies and all the processes involved.

Our interviewees recommend looking at what the concepts of diversity, equity and inclusion mean within your organization. Some companies do not know what diversity and inclusion imply. Thus, it is crucial to work out these concepts as precisely as possible by asking questions such as: What exactly does 'feeling at home' mean? What would this mean for each individual within the organization?

Diversity recruiter Nezahat Yildirim explains: "What do we understand by 'diversity and inclusion'? Why is it so important for our organization? What do we need to be more diverse- and for whom?"

Some confusion also arises around the concepts of equality and equity. Equity plays into unequal positions, something the principle of 'equal treatment' does not. Hanan Challouki explains, "CEO's often put in a diversity statement that all their employees are equal or treated equally. But some people need more than others because of a socially unequal position. For example, a separate track for people with fewer educational opportunities is not equal – because not every employee has a right to follow that track – but it is equitable and therefore necessary to become more inclusive. This means that sometimes you have to invest more and in different ways to suit everyone's needs."

After you have defined what the concepts of diversity, equity and inclusion mean within your organizational context, it is vital to set goals. These goals within diversity policies are important for having a vision of the future and holding onto it. Employees need different types of motivations to want to commit to DEI. This way, you define values and goals for your organization to include the various types of employees and to work together towards an equitable work environment.

Several interviewees recommend formulating values to provide even more clarity and establish what you stand for as an organization. Manuela Kalsky, Professor of Theology and Society, recommends arriving at those values by first asking colleagues what they find *valuable,* so that it is not just about abstract *values.* It is impossible to make everyone feel at home, but by having an in-depth conversation with everyone, you can more consciously arrive at a set of shared values.

Our interviewees warned against focusing too much on a paper policy, which could conceal what's happening in reality. Still, a concrete policy is vital to link time and money to it, as well as ensuring that it does not remain in the hands of one or a few pioneers. Bouchra Talidi spends a lot of time on finalizing a consultancy project with an organization: "I want to make sure that when I'm gone, someone takes my place and that inclusive working and selection become routine. I lay the foundation, but after that, it's up to the organization itself."

It is crucial to infuse all departments and processes with diversity, equity and inclusion. That may also mean tearing down some departments or functions entirely and rebuilding them. Diversity practitioners discussed different roadmaps to guide change processes. Joy Lodarmasse used an able-bodied body as a metaphor to describe the different departments and processes within large organizations in light of DEI. In a nutshell, the head is the top of the organization; the arms are the company's business; and the legs are HR and the communication department and the work culture of an organization. Diversity practitioners cited that policies must seep into all layers of an organization; this can only be done by looking at processes and structures and involving everyone.

HOW TO SUSTAIN

Endurance is key to running any marathon, so in the last part of this chapter, we'll take you through how to sustain working on DEI. The format "start – build – sustain" is not chronological but dynamic. Maintaining and making a success of the change process toward a more diverse and equitable organization requires recruitment, selection and an inclusive work culture. Recruitment and selection alone are not enough; that usually leads to equally rapid employee recruitment and departures. Organizational culture is crucial in making diversity policies more sustainable.

Recruitment and selection

The first question employers should ask themselves is: Why do we want to become 'more diverse'? "Usually, the answer I get is that they want to be a reflection of society to meet the needs of their customers better. But they are often less able to define those needs, so they don't actually know what competencies new staff members should have," says Siham Ammal, consultant and trainer in diversity and inclusion.

Recruiting more diversely requires you to properly map out which personnel you are missing and why. In every organization, (un)conscious exclusion takes place. Are you prepared to face up to the exclusion within your company, take the time to reflect and then take action? Melek Usta, founder of recruitment agency *Colorful People*, gives an example: "If the analysis of your workforce shows, for example, that there are few people over 50 in service and further investigation reveals that age discrimination underlies this, then you must be brave enough to recruit people based on that information."

Our interviewees advise thinking about more than what you need as a company. Above all else, what makes your organization attractive to potential employees? Alliander, the energy network company where Joy Lodarmasse is the manager of diversity and inclusion, already needs to seem appealing due to staff shortages. "For example, if you are a refugee from Syria and you did a technical training there or had a technical job, you get Dutch lessons from us, you can retake your diploma in the Netherlands, you can get your driver's license, you get a job guarantee – you get it all. We have to be an attractive employer for all potential talent. You then learn to think from the potential employee's point of view."

Next, we'll delve deeper into the advice and experiences of diversity practitioners on aspects of the selection process. People have many biases that play a role in the recruitment and selection process. Our interviewees argue for more objective selection and reducing bias in the recruitment and selection process by, among other things, involving more people in the application process. It is also essential to closely examine your preconceptions and selection criteria. What are the most important competencies per position? And do you really select for those skills? Elsa van de Loo observes: "Go through the profiles of all the people you have hired and rejected, and see if there is a pattern. Often, quite surprising analyses come out of that."

Letting go of the work journey candidates must have traveled is also crucial in the selection process. People can develop competencies differently; not every student can afford to go on an internship abroad. Siham Ammal, diversity advisor, explains: "Candidates with a migration background are more likely to have cared for family members, teaching them independence; that's a skill. Or perhaps you think an internship abroad is important because it shows that someone can deal well with different cultures. Growing up in certain parts of Amsterdam, you also had to deal with many different cultures."

Another part of the selection process is the job posting. Organizations that want to recruit more diversely will miss the mark if they do not sufficiently adapt their texts for job openings. Therefore, our interviewees advise companies to be open to applicants from different functions or fields. Companies can simply state this in the job posting, focusing on the required competencies instead of years of work experience within a particular role and not using too much technical jargon. Nezahat Yildirim notes, "What strikes me is that most vacancies are written for the departing colleague."

Some other recommendations from our interviewees are to not list too many job requirements and to think carefully about the 'experience required'. Potential candidates' needs must also be considered and included in the job description. Joy Lodarmasse notes: "It is important to know what people are looking for in their job and what they expect in terms of opportunities from their employer. For example, one candidate is looking for a permanent position and growth opportunities; the other wants training opportunities and a sports membership. Be concrete and clear about this in your job postings and ask new colleagues what appealed to them in these descriptions."

The diversity statement in job postings 'We think diversity is important...' is a recurring dilemma. Shervin Nekuee emphasizes, "Avoid 'diversity is a party' texts that walk off the privilege of the dominant group." It is better to clearly explain why you, as an organization, want to be diverse and inclusive and link this to your company's story.

An attractive job posting based on competencies and an in-depth interview with potential candidates is the way to go. Our interviewees also recommend that the selection not be done by one person. Nezahat Yildirim observes: "The selection of candidates is fairer if you have several evaluators, preferably from different positions. It is important that they first assess separately and then discuss how everyone came to their assessment. A selection never becomes completely objective, but it does become more objective through this approach."

During the job interview, the focus should be on the applicant's story. The people conducting the interview must be well-prepared and consciously deal with their own biases and thinking patterns. "And for heaven's sake, don't focus on making a personal connection with the applicant," says Elsa van de Loo, "When you want to become more diverse and inclusive as an organization, then you want to change. If you're mainly looking for a personal connection at first sight, then chances are you'll hire someone who looks and thinks just like you."

Our interviewees indicated that having an eye for individual needs of new colleagues entering the work place is very important as an employer. Here again, you have the difference between equality and equity.

– Equality is: all new colleagues receive the same support.
– Equity is: all new colleagues receive support tailored to their wishes and needs.

Mentoring can help new employees get to know the organization, but this should be for everyone, and people should be able to develop themselves as individuals in their own way. The danger of mentoring is that people can be shaped by the system and lose their individuality. Because of this, such mentoring programs can also hold back change within the organization's structures. Astrid Elburg, leadership consultant, explains, "Coupling a mentor to someone often results in this person adopting the mentor's behavior. This removes their opportunity to show their potential. Also, making their way in an organization as their authentic self is more difficult."

One possible solution is equivalent mentoring programs. "Often new, young employees are paired with an older employee, and the latter shows the newcomer how everything works. However, there also needs to be room for younger employees to encourage those older ones to come out of their comfort zones. New colleagues must hold you up to that mirror of self-reflection. This is also called reverse mentoring," Professor Halleh Ghorashi explains.

When colleagues are promoted to other or higher positions within your organization, it is vital that you again look closely at the competencies needed for a job and not only rely on recognition and connection. Siham Ammal summarizes this issue: "A manager recognizes talent faster when he recognizes himself in his team members, thereby creating a pool of people who all look alike. So, looking at talent more inclusively is essential."

When it comes to outflow, exit interviews are an indispensable element if you want to become more diverse and inclusive as an organization. "Which employees don't feel like they belong?" is discovered during the departure process. Professor of Diversity Halleh Ghorashi explains: "Exit interviews are very suitable for uncovering the organization's blind spots and helping to discover what's transpiring between the lines; this often remains hidden. You can use the information from those conversations to make executives aware of the dynamics within the organization: why do people leave and what drives people to stay?"

The house rules: scrutinizing work culture

Our interviewees indicated that workplace culture is a hugely important factor in sustaining change in diversity, equity and inclusion. If you want to work toward an inclusive work environment, it is crucial to be aware that your organization also has:
1. a specific work culture and group formation with written and unwritten rules
2. a norm, which means that employees who fall outside and (visibly) deviate from this norm face prejudice and experience exclusion.

Organizational leadership and employees need to be aware of the work culture and how it needs to change. Shervin Nekuee emphasizes: "Ensuring a safe work environment starts with having conversations about your organization's culture and making this as tangible as possible."

Bettina Haarbosch, D&I Program Manager at the Dutch Railways (NS), touches on another critical element of organizational culture: the safety of speaking up. "At NS, we facilitate 'the uncomfortable conversation' at different levels of the organization. That goes beyond diversity and inclusion. It's about ethics and having a moral compass. If you have a culture of judgment or a culture of fear, are people going to challenge you?"

Inclusivity researcher Onur Şahin points out that it is also important to be mindful of invisible diversity. "Some employees dare to make these characteristics visible and discuss them, but more often they hide them because there are stigmas attached to them: for example, with mental disorders, political preferences, sexual orientation or religion. When managers ignore these hidden differences, it impacts performance but more importantly impacts the employee's health, both physically and mentally."

Marianne Dijkshoorn, a consultant on accessibility and inclusion, also says that employers aren't always considerate toward employees with physical or mental disabilities. "Employers are quick to think, 'If I hire you, how does that work? Do I have to change and adapt the building?' There is a lot of ambiguity about this, although the corona crisis has shown how easily we can collaborate from home. Employers should look into this and ask questions to the employee – this person often knows what's needed, and it doesn't have to be as much as you think. I believe that communication would help bring more clarity in these situations."

Inequality – discrimination

Taking Article 1 of the Dutch Constitution as a starting point for your diversity policy is only meaningful if you actually dare to live up to this principle of equity with respect for people's different (life) experiences. This requires the courage to look in the mirror and investigate inequity. Marieke van der Brink, Professor of Gender and Diversity notes: "That means that as a CEO, as the initiator of this process, you will also make yourself unpopular with some colleagues. That's part of the process."

Countering discrimination and inequality requires structures and procedures to support a safe work environment. Thus, according to Geraldine Moodley, international adviser on inclusive leadership, setting up a legally sound grievance structure within organizations is essential. You need to, at least, get these questions right, Geraldine Moodley explains: "How do you identify the grounds and forms of discrimination? Is there a grievance structure in place, and are employees encouraged to actually use it? How do you handle the complaints? In what way do you assist someone? What is your communication cycle? How do you deal with this until the end without passing it off to a confidant?"

Leadership

Shaping an inclusive work environment requires inclusive leadership. According to our interviewees, this is so essential that we could easily fill a whole book with their knowledge on the subject. In *The Inclusion Marathon*, we limit ourselves to one chapter: *The Manager*.

In this chapter, we summarize their most important advice and experiences. This section reflects on why inclusive leadership is so essential. Terence Guiamo says: "An organizational culture is formed by the people who work in a company. It concerns people, and I believe that you have to start with the leader's actions." Esther Mollema, a leadership coach, concludes that organizations should include inclusive skills as an essential part of a leader's package. "Executives who may be good at the task at hand but have no aptitude for inclusive leadership and don't want to become more inclusive should no longer be able to move on so easily."

Measuring diversity and inclusion

Several diversity practitioners say it is crucial to measure diversity and inclusion to uncover how an organization is doing in this area. But numbers and research are no silver bullet. Most interviewees indicated that employee satisfaction surveys can be an essential source of information, with the caveat that you can never rule out employees filling in (socially) desirable answers when a work culture is unsafe. The anonymity and design of such a survey are therefore paramount.[22]

Additionally, it is a good idea to follow up on these surveys with in-depth interviews to gain deeper insight and understanding into why employees feel at home or not. Onur Şahin says it's important to tailor the measurement of diversity and inclusion to your organization's context and goals. "An example: we want at least ten percent of our new hires to have a certain minority characteristic. In addition to such factual statistics, you also need to measure more human-based aspects by asking employees about inclusion, for instance by an anonymous questionnaire. Then you can determine if things are actually changing and if the policies you want to implement are reflected in your employees' experiences."

Our interviewees indicated that registering minority characteristics can make it clear at a glance how homogeneous a company still is but take into account the anonymity and carefulness of this data.

The Manager

"With great power comes great responsibility." –
Ben Parker tells his nephew Peter Parker, also known as Spider-Man, in Stan Lee's *Spider-Man* comics

This quote summarizes the essence of our interviewees' insights when it comes to inclusive leadership. American diversity practitioner Farzin Farzad specializes in power and power relations. In his work, he refers to different power relations and how these have been unequal in gender, gender identity, skin color, origin, socioeconomic background, sexual orientation and disabilities. Farzin Farzad says: "You receive that kind of power without effort. When you possess this power, you are responsible for creating power for those with less power and whose voices are often left unheard. Because of this historically grown inequality, we have developed a tendency to consider the views and opinions of white, upper-class males as the norm or the truth. Voices representing marginalized groups are regarded, for example, as the 'Asian, Black or Muslim perspective'."

In (public) spaces, the dominance of certain voices has existed for centuries. Farzin Farzad emphasizes that when you hold power based on unequal power relations, your voice is more likely to be heard. It automatically reaches further and gains more weight. Of course, you did not choose to receive these privileges, but you can decide how to use them. Farzin Farzad explains: "You can't surrender your power, but you can take responsibility for sharing your power by creating spaces to which more people have access and where everyone can share the space with you equally."

This chapter will unravel these privileges and power relations around leadership. We will discuss this in the context of inclusive workplaces in the Netherlands. Unfortunately, there is no roadmap to solving inequality within power dynamics. However, as clearly as possible, we compiled our interviewees' experiences and insights on leadership within three segments: how to start, how to build and how to sustain, as in the previous chapter *The Organization*.

HOW TO START

Inclusive leadership is defined by leaders who are aware of their power and privileges. All interviewees agree managers should not shy away from difficult situations and should offer support to employees who raise issues of discrimination and abuse of power. Fatima Elatik experienced the consequences of leadership based on fear of change during her political career as a local politician. She now works as a strategic advisor for governmental agencies. "Managers must realize that becoming more diverse is not a fun process. It means bringing in people with different perspectives, methods and ways of working. That requires quite a bit of change management skills," Fatima urges.

On top of that, a manager must be brave enough to look in the mirror and observe their reflection. Self-reflection is complicated and painful but necessary for an inclusive leader. Bouchra Talidi, the owner of Inclusioncy, explains: "As a manager, you need to get to know yourself really well and examine your own unconscious biases." Hanan Challouki, the founder of Inclusified, insists on listening to and collaborating with others. This includes creating a safe working environment and capitalizing on everyone's qualities and experiences. So, use your employees' vision, knowledge and talent. An inclusive leader is open to different perspectives; it takes time and energy, but focusing only on a quick result often hinders the inclusion of these different perspectives. Pursuing these viewpoints requires leaders who dare to ask (personal) questions. In doing so, managers must allow others to be vulnerable without judging their mistakes.

Therefore, it should become common practice to reward managers for the aspects of inclusive leadership mentioned above and not just because they met specific targets. Mohan Verstegen, policy advisor and doctor at the Dutch Defense Department, emphasizes that people-oriented rewards should be the way to go to encourage inclusive leadership. "Rewards are often task-oriented: you either have met a production target or built a new system. Employees rarely receive rewards for people-oriented work, e.g., intervening when bullying occurs in the workplace."

Our interviewees notice that organizations often push emotion aside to meet targets and deliver products under time pressure. The lack of focus on empathy usually involves controlling employees and using excessive methods to observe them; these include performance reviews, checking achieved targets, etc. Reaching all the targets becomes the primary goal, often at the expense of our humanity. But luckily, times are changing because employees yearn for more trust and compassion on the job, as this makes them happier and feel more at home.

Inclusivity researcher Onur Şahin states that today's work experience is more relational than rational. "To keep the peace within teams while also thinking about achieving goals, a leader should be part of the team. For that, one needs empathy. It's more than just delegating tasks." Having no room for vulnerability can have far-reaching consequences for the work atmosphere and employees. This shortage stems from a fear of change or of making mistakes and being judged harshly for them. Karima El Bouchtaoui, diversity consultant and Director at Ocullus Consultancy, strongly encourages being vulnerable and deepening relationships, especially regarding diversity and inclusion. "We often think we are different because we react to external differences. But the only way to get past that is by breaking the barrier and being vulnerable."

HOW TO BUILD

Self-reflection, vulnerability and compassion are essential for shaping a safe workplace under inclusive leadership. But how do you build this safe workplace environment? Halleh Ghorashi is a Professor of Diversity at Vrije Universiteit Amsterdam. She refers to developing a third eye and ear to see qualities that are often hidden and to pay attention to differences and inequality within your team: "Let go of your possible biases and look deeper."

Without these extra senses, executives fail to see their colleagues' or customers' needs and get stuck in fear-based choices that stem from conscious and unconscious biases. Esther Mollema, best-selling author and expert on entrepreneurship and leadership, explains that understanding how the brain works can help correct one's preconceptions. "Only then can you look more deeply at an employee's qualities and ensure that people don't have to conform to your idea of the norm when working with you."

Our main question remains: How do you contribute to a safe working environment as a manager? To answer this question, start by exploring what a safe work environment means within your organization or team. Interviewees reveal descriptions such as feeling at home and being yourself. However, creating a safe work environment requires the courage to accept that within your organization or team there is a certain standard, a specific work culture and exclusion mechanisms at work. You can't provide safety if you don't carefully map out these issues within your organization.

Onur Şahin, researcher on inclusion in the workplace, says: "There is always a certain culture and norm within an organiza-tion. The workforce often changes when organizations become more diverse, but the work culture remains the same. As a manager, you must be aware of that and play a principal role in that change." When training managers, Esther Mollema asks them the following questions to map their workplace culture with their team members: How do we use humor, and is it hostile toward others? How do we divide the tasks? Does everyone believe this process is fair?

As a manager, you act as a role model for the group. Your behavior affects the atmosphere within the team and how employees behave among themselves and toward you. There-fore, managers should always be mindful of employees who belong to the marginalized group because how they act toward these groups will often be perpetuated by other employees. Siela Ardjosemito-Jethoe, policy advisor on diversity and inclusion, refers to emotional labor[23] that people from marginalized groups must do to survive in the workplace: "It can take a lot of energy for them to hold their own in a heteronormative, white, masculine work environment. For example, they are constantly faced with questions about their background or way of life or are confronted with prejudices about their lifestyle. This constant questioning can be a heavy burden to carry. To take away that emotional labor, managers must keep a close eye on such dynamics and on their own behavior as well."

Moreover, two additional components often (unintentionally) lead to exclusion within the workplace, namely humor and staff outings. Humor is a double-edged sword; it can be a great tool to create a common identity and forge relationships within a group. However, it can also be a type that not everyone likes or just isn't funny. Misplaced jokes tend to lean toward exclusion, bullying and discrimination. Thus, humor can include but also exclude people.[24] In other words, humor is necessary to ensure a safe atmosphere, but humor can also create an unsafe work environment.

Inclusivity researcher Onur Şahin describes humor's complicated and paradoxical function in the workplace. "Especially as a manager, you must be aware of the role that jokes can play in the extent to which your colleagues feel at home in your team. Do you think all jokes are permissible or not?" The leader's responsibility is to explore the boundaries of what is funny and what is not. And remember: racist or sexist humor in the workplace usually goes against local and federal laws.

Other aspects that often exclude people in many organizations and companies are staff outings and informal get-togethers. These play an essential role in the formation of (work) relationships. On these occasions, people get to know each other and share positive and negative experiences concerning the workplace. And it is only fair for every colleague to access these formal and informal outings. Inclusive staff meetings are thus extremely crucial. Terence Guiamo, Global Director of Inclusion, Diversity & Belonging at Just Eat Takeaway, shares an example: "There should be some variety in these get-togethers: should it always be a get-together at the same ski location? At least make sure that non-alcoholic drinks are also served, such as virgin cocktails."

HOW TO SUSTAIN

How does a manager preserve a safe work environment? All interviewees mentioned the importance of really listening and taking the time to curtail assumptions. In addition, diversity practitioners stress the importance of asking questions rather than assuming things. The intention might be good, but if you don't take the time to ask questions, you make decisions based on assumptions. Gatra Peshtaz advises organizations on including refugees in the workplace. She recalls an example of an employer with good intentions. This employer had created a halal corner with a separate sandwich machine for a Syrian colleague without asking what the employee wanted and needed. A previous Muslim colleague of Syrian origin had appreciated this gesture. Gatra Peshtaz explains: "I had a counseling session with this new Syrian employee who indicated he didn't need a separate sandwich machine. In turn, this 'gift' made him feel like he was not part of the group, thus leaving the employer confused. 'Is it Muslim light now? Beer or no beer?' Your intentions might be good, but if you don't take the time to ask questions, you may easily make decisions based on assumptions."

Both an employee and an employer bear responsibility in these situations. The Syrian-Dutch employee could also have indicated that he doesn't need a separate sandwich machine. Still, you have more power in the relationship as a manager or employer. You must contribute to a safe working environment by setting an example for all your employees. This example also demonstrates the importance of avoiding generalized assumptions about certain groups, such as Muslims or Syrians, as there is, of course, a lot of diversity within groups.

In brief, a leader should ask questions and dare to start the conversation on diversity, equity and inclusion, thus making room for discomfort and conflict. As poet and philosopher, Audre Lorde once said: "It is not our differences that divide us, but our inability to recognize, accept and celebrate these differences."[25]

When you get in touch with stories or perspectives that are different from your own, or sometimes even the opposite of your beliefs, it can cause discomfort and conflict. In an inclusive work environment, colleagues should learn to deal with these distressing feelings. Or, as Terence Guiamo states, "getting more comfortable with the uncomfortable." The starting point here is to practice examining and reflecting on your way of life, perspectives and stories and, as a result, discover that your story is part of a bigger picture. In short: your thoughts and ideas do not apply to everyone. The manager plays an important role in accepting this and letting go of normative beliefs.

Halleh Ghorashi advises leaders to create 'in-between spaces' where they try to put their truths and opinions aside as much as possible and listen to others with an open mind.[26] "Suspend your opinion for a moment to make room for the other person's story. As soon as you feel the connection, space opens up for your story. This in-between allows both parties to step into that space at the same time, without judgment, opinion or expectation." Sharing stories is about emotions and conversations on what touches people, which is often not fully encouraged within the workplace.

Leaders should know that people communicate differently when conversing with others, e.g., introverts versus extroverts. Also, being aware of your communication style as a leader and not imposing it on your team members is a crucial aspect of inclusive leadership. That is why Elsa van de Loo sometimes prefers to train employees and managers separately in her training course *Selecting without prejudice*. "In my experience, people don't always speak out when their manager is present. Thus, it is sometimes essential to separate executives and employees in complex conversations or meetings, so that everyone dares to speak up," Elsa van de Loo clarifies.

A manager should remain aware of exclusion and (social and historically grown) inequality that have repercussions on behavior and dealings in the workplace. Farzin Farzad gently reminds everyone to stay aware of their privileges. "The tricky thing about privilege is that you are often unaware that you have it. It's all about what you do with it when someone points out your privilege. Consider it a gift when someone bothers to point out a short-sighted or offensive comment."

As a team leader, it is important to realize that uncomfortable conversations often involve asking members of marginalized groups to be open about their personal experiences of discrimination. However, this is an unfair expectation and asks a lot from those affected. Another way to do this is to hire a professional who is willing to share their story; it is not easy to do, and it takes a lot of energy. People who are willing and able to do this should get financial compensation. Providing education and teaching people to eliminate their prejudices is a sincere profession and not something people should be doing in their free time.

Finally, a leader should manage conflict by empathizing and bringing people closer together. Diversity practitioner Geraldine Moodley, sums it up: "Being able to deal with conflict fearlessly makes you a leader. And it is precisely in teams that are or become diverse that disputes arise more often. There is nothing wrong with that – it is healthy – but you have to deal with these frictions as a manager."

Geraldine Moodley herself has often given training in conflict management and explains that it revolves around questions such as: "How do you deal with conflict without feeling attacked yourself? Do you manage to be open to perspectives other than your own? Can you deal with the emotions that conflict brings? Conflict management involves teaching people to deal with sadness, anger and other emotions." According to several of our interviewees, conflict management is essential to creating a safe work environment as a manager, and it should be a fundamental part of their training and skill set.

The Diversity Practitioner

Diversity practitioners focus on changing organizational structures and habits, broadening ingrained thought patterns. This does not always make them well-liked by colleagues in the workplace. Questioning what is 'normal' requires courageous professionals who know themselves inside and out, and who can deal with resistance to change and discomfort. Our interviewees search for abuse of power, discrimination and exclusion in order to create the safest possible working environment for every employee. However, this is not always appreciated by managers and employees who belong to the dominant group.

As Sara Ahmed describes in her book *On Being Included*: "pointing out discriminatory behavior can make employees who belong to a certain norm feel 'unsafe'."[27] The paradox is that they feel also unsafe, just as the person who has undergone discrimination. However, because of historical inequity, workplaces can be still more concerned with the feelings of unsafety of the person who discriminates than of the person who is discriminated against. The DEI field is also relatively new, making it more likely that doubts about the diversity practitioner's approach and abilities will arise. This chapter also consists of the parts: how to start, how to build and how to sustain. Again, all the pillars described should exist side by side.

HOW TO START

Several interviewees indicated that they had transformed their experiences of exclusion into expertise. They learned to use their personal experiences in a focused way to support other people's learning process. These experiences make you a more empathetic diversity practitioner and increase your commitment to the profession. "It gives you extra intrinsic motivation, ensuring you keep up this complicated profession. Using your own experiences with discrimination and exclusion is powerful. Still, one should be careful, in case deep wounds have not yet healed," Jeftha Pattikawa, Program Director at the National Archives, explains.

The starting point for an inclusive work environment is self-knowledge for employees and managers. That means it's especially important for the diversity practitioner. When we asked about a diversity practitioner's job profile, self-knowledge was featured as an essential skill. Below, we construct the job profile for a diversity practitioner based on our interviewees' points of view.

The Job Profile: A driven seducer with (self-) knowledge and a bird's-eye view

1. Know yourself. The diversity practitioner must reflect on their prejudices and sensitivities in order to guide others. Marten Bos, a freelance diversity trainer, explains: "Knowing myself also means knowing my privileges, sensitivities and triggers."
2. The diversity practitioner is a connector of different perspectives and must be able to deal and connect with different people. Bouchra Talidi, the owner of Inclusioncy, comments: "You have to be willing to listen to people who are not like you and have differing ideas."
3. The diversity practitioner must be able to oversee the entire organization. Yet there must be a balance between being an insider and an outsider, which is quite tricky. A certain distance is necessary to monitor from a bird's-eye view. Lawyer and trainer Elsa van de Loo says that maintaining a distance also means giving people space to discover something for themselves. "In my training courses, I give suggestions to get people thinking. It's not up to me as a trainer to give my own opinion, as I hope to get other perspectives from the group."
4. You must not be afraid to hold up a mirror to yourself and others. The diversity practitioner must be able to put themselves in the mindset of others, especially individuals who have not had

to think much about DEI. This understanding requires being able to withstand backlash and keep pushing to get through to people. Esther Mollema, leadership expert and coach, confirms: "You have to start the conversation with people at the top of organizations and society, who have a worldview that has never been challenged. It's your job to tell them that they don't necessarily know everything and help them understand what is really going on in society and in the workplace."

5. The diversity practitioner must possess many types of knowledge, including sociology, psychology, theology, anthropology, colonialism and power relations. Joan Tol, expert in change management, adds: "As a diversity practitioner, you learn to motivate, to enthuse and to influence. It is also vital to know how change processes work. And it would be best if you also had a good dose of resilience. Once you understand how change management works, you'll be more aware of the fact that you will encounter resistance."[28]

6. The diversity practitioner has to be able to seduce people to change (the organization) and bring them toward realizing a common dream for the future. A strong belief in the added value of diversity is necessary to get people on board. Or as diversity consultant and advisor at Pharos, Kaveh Bouteh, describes, "A diversity practitioner must be someone who sees embracing diversity and inclusion not as a burden but as a joy. Someone who is unafraid of the unknown, wants to meet different people and takes the time to do so."

Diversity practitioners, according to the outside world

Diversity practitioners deal with personal experiences, prejudice, exclusion and resistance every day. Because diversity, equity and inclusion often evoke negative connotations and reactions, employees refuse to engage in conversation with some of our interviewees. So, diversity practitioners are also pigeonholed because of the sensitive nature of the work; they are not always appreciated or taken seriously.

The diversity practitioner is regularly the messenger of uncomfortable and painful news. And for that message of change to land more gently, it helps if people like you. But even the most happy-go-lucky diversity practitioners are occasionally seen as killjoys. The 'feminist killjoy' and 'institutional killjoy' are terms from Sara Ahmed's work.[29] She uses them to describe employees who spoil the party or kill the joy with their critical reflection on power dynamics within organizations. Jeftha Pattikawa says, "You're constantly questioning the status quo. So, the fact that people look a bit nervous when you enter a meeting room is part of the job." Professor of Gender and Diversity Marieke van den Brink notes that it is challenging to fulfill this role. Therefore, some diversity practitioners choose (sometimes out of necessity) a softer approach. This is also known as being a tempered radical in the scientific literature.[30] The professor illustrates, "Those who denounce inequality are often unpopular and thus hit a wall. This can incite them to take on a tempered role because being 'the radical' is deemed too tough. They then try to keep it fun and positive to get people on board. However, inequality is not all fun and games."

The different types of diversity practitioners: What roles do diversity practitioners currently fulfill in the Dutch DEI field?

1. The experts.
    – Chief Diversity Officers: manage their departments and have high positions within the organizational structure, including decision-making power
    – Independent consultants: often have been advising different organizations and guide from the outside
    – Diversity Officers within the organization: responsible for diversity policy but carry it out from middle- or lower-management positions within their company

2. Employees with diversity, equity and inclusion as a task in their job description, which is most common in HR departments, making an HR employee take on diversity as one of their many tasks.
3. Ambassadors.
   – Employees who –find diversity essential – often from their own experiences with exclusion – and try to call attention to the subject within their organizations
   – Members of a diversity action group: employees involved with the issue who try to push change as part of an action group
   – Top managers who put the issue on the agenda at a high level and pave the way for professionals within the organization to realize implementation plans

The pitfall of having a separate diversity department or professional within the organization, or the unfortunate fact that the issue can end up solely with HR, is that everything falls on them. Organizational anthropologist Danielle Braun confirms this: "We have to be careful of that because DEI is part of the whole organization."[31]

Internal or external diversity practitioner?

We interviewed diversity practitioners who advise organizations both internally and externally. As expected, the opinions differ. Overall, however, the best of both worlds, or a holistic approach, seems to be the way to get DEI started within an organization. Terence Guiamo led diversity departments in several places. Currently, he does so at Just Eat Takeaway. He sees significant benefits to working from inside an organization in a permanent position on diversity and inclusion. "The considerable advantage of an internal role is that you know the organization and people well. You can sometimes create awareness and get things done a little easier. Additionally, decision-making power and support from the top can help you take a critical stance. As an external consultant, it's all temporary. Sometimes, you might not want to lose your assignment, and that fear can play a role in how critical you are."

On the other hand, inclusive recruitment trainer Siham Ammal experienced that the need for DEI didn't immediately catch on as an internal advisor: "I think that sometimes you are taken more seriously as a self-employed professional or someone from outside than when you work within an organization. Sometimes the message seems more acceptable from the outside than from the inside."

As a common thread, we see that external consultants or researchers mainly play a role in launching diversity, equity and inclusion through advice, training, scans or temporary projects. In addition, they play an important role as experts and advisors who are used strategically by permanent diversity staff when there is a need for guidance within their organization.

HOW TO BUILD

How is a task set up and implemented? What projects do our interviewees accept or not accept – and why? And how do they influence how the assignment takes shape? The diversity practitioners we spoke to all agree that they need freedom when taking on a project. It's their job to (co-)construct and figure out what's happening within a company. Working toward more diverse and inclusive workplaces requires commitment from the beginning, preferably from professionals who know what they're doing. They are trained to assess the organization and the issues at hand and plan a straightforward approach.

Our interviewees draw up several preconditions for whether to accept a task, and they have different methods to determine if a company is a good fit. Most diversity practitioners count on top management's total commitment and authentic intentions. Also, there must be a significant amount of leeway to genuinely carry out the task. Geraldine Moodley, inclusive leadership consultant and adviser, emphasizes the importance of trust from management: "My mandate has to come from the CEO, who also gives me carte blanche." Hanan Challouki, expert on inclusive communication, adds, "I can't work on diversity and inclusion if I'm constantly being tapped on the shoulder. I need to be able to work independently. A company that wants to work on diversity and inclusion but still wants to micromanage everything will not get the right results."

Diversity practitioners also try to assess how much diversity an organization or team can handle. They describe this as getting to know the *diversity level*. Asking employees what they understand by 'diversity and inclusion' and how they notice it in their daily work can already estimate the level of diversity awareness within the group. There is a big difference between awareness and working with concrete tools to bring about change.

Approaching an assignment

There is no standard approach but what emerged as a general denominator from our interviews is that diversity practitioners often start their assignment with an inventory of what is happening within a specific organization. This inventory usually consists of one or more inclusion/exclusion scans, interviews with various employees throughout the company and a mapping out of the organization's hierarchy, departments and processes. This registration process is followed by examining what approaches and interventions could benefit organizations, departments and teams. An example of this is Shervin Nekuee's four pillars:
- Analyzing the individual level of knowledge of the field of diversity and inclusion
- Mapping out the work culture and exclusion mechanisms
- Critically examining existing methods such as recruitment, transfers, departures
- Inclusive leadership: uncovering the coaching needs of a manager

Jeftha Pattikawa indicates that diversity practitioners should always ask themselves this question: "What is the effect I want to bring about?" They can achieve results in different ways; sometimes you give space within the company, and sometimes you have to take the helm. Sometimes you have to find partners to walk the DEI path. In any case, there is certainly no fixed road map," Jeftha Pattikawa illustrates.

Awareness, resistance and discomfort make DEI more complex than other organizational issues because inequality has been historically brought about within society. Siham Achahboun, Program Manager of Cultural Diversity at insurance company Achmea, says: "It's about unconscious processes that we often don't even know exist, making it much more personal and complex than most practical organizational changes." As diversity practitioner Marten Bos explains, resistance can also be a good starting point: "It may not always be the easiest energy to work with, but it is better than no energy at all. I also try to listen carefully to the stories that arise from resistance, then the emotions and sentiments are quickly released."

So resistance is often a conversation starter, but some people just don't want to go along with it. This is when our interviewees try to be realistic and focus on getting as many people along as possible without hoping to convince everyone. Esther Mollema, a leadership expert, refers to those who refuse to accept change in the chapter *The Organization*. Her advice is to focus most of your energy on DEI drivers to bring more people along the ride.

The diversity practitioners recommend building ambassador networks, such as sounding boards, diversity networks or action groups. These networks can support organizational change in DEI because diversity practitioners or departments cannot do it alone. They can function as a safe space where employees who have experienced exclusion can share their experiences and learn from each other. Diversity practitioner Bouchra Talidi indicates that we must support these networks with knowledge and tools and shouldn't expect voluntary commitment. Employees need time and energy to work on this complex issue, so extra hours

– during working hours – and a training budget are needed. "In the beginning, when I set up such a network, participation was still voluntary. Fortunately, that has changed. You have to create time for this. That gives such a network even more reason to exist. Slowly but surely, this network gains a real voice within the organization, and they get a seat at the table at the top," Bouchra Talidi clarifies.

Sharing your personal story and connecting stories by looking for similarities in experiences is a powerful way to practice listening to each other. Engaging in dialogue with one another increases the involvement of employees around diversity issues. Halleh Ghorashi, Professor of Diversity and Integration, calls it looking for the space between yourself and others.

"Just because you've eaten couscous or spicy food doesn't mean you understand everything about multiculturalism. Nor does it mean that you understand the pain of refugees when you have not experienced it yourself. To grasp how the other person feels, you have to be willing to step out of your own world for a moment and listen to the other person," says Gatra Peshtaz, advisor on refugee participation in the workplace.

HOW TO SUSTAIN

In the final part of this chapter, we discuss how our interviewees persevere by being satisfied with small steps and forming networks to exchange knowledge and experiences. Finally, we go into the (non)sense of establishing a professional code or quality label.

In a field where you often have to deal with resistance and the excesses of historical inequality, being happy with small successes is essential to taking more significant steps and making issues more concrete eventually. "People are sometimes good at making things complex with all sorts of models and visuals. If you take small steps, you eventually contribute to big steps", states Nicole Reimink-Böttger, Head of Diversity and Inclusion at ABN AMRO Bank.

Having your safety net is an important part of withstanding the hardships of diversity work. Joan Tol quotes the DEI coach and writer Grethe van Geffen, "Take care of yourself because you are in a field that is not easy. It's so layered and the issues are sometimes so complex. Plus, you can't always make the impact and the difference you want to. Many D&I professionals are burned out after three years or so, if they're unaware of this and don't protect themselves." It is up to diversity practitioners to build this network to prevent complete burnout within a few years.

Opinions among diversity practitioners are divided about establishing a code or hallmark. Currently, there are no codes, labels, unions or professional associations in the DEI field in the Netherlands. The question that diversity practitioners ask themselves is: Who determines what quality is? Even so, they believe DEI deserves a hallmark because of its social importance. The Dutch Railways (NS) program manager at Bettina Haarbosch: "It's mainly about creating a moral compass. It concerns Article 1 of our constitution: you shall not discriminate. Maybe we can get inspired by the Dutch Journalism Code. It's definitely worth thinking about."

Diversity consultant Karima el Bouchtaoui describes the DEI field as a profusion of diversity practitioners with different qualities. "That's difficult to capture under one label." Halleh Ghorashi offers a more community-based solution called *horizontal learning networks*. In such a network, practical knowledge (diversity practitioners), scientific knowledge (researchers) and experiential knowledge (employees within organizations) are shared and connected on a level playing field. "I think we would benefit from a horizontal learning network, where everyone working on diversity issues can learn from each other. There is a lot of practical experience from diversity practitioners, there are personal experiences of employees working on diversity issues, and there is more and more scientific research. It would be nice if we could connect this practical, scientific and experiential knowledge in an equal learning network."

Knowledge is Power

We ended the previous chapter, *The Diversity Practitioner,* with Professor Halleh Ghorashi's idea of establishing a horizontal learning network to connect practical, scientific and experiential knowledge. A valuable question arises within many fields: how is the science related to the practice? Especially when working toward more DEI-oriented workplaces, linking science to practice is challenging at times. After all, scientific knowledge is also bound by norms and partly founded on historical inequality. As a result, scientific knowledge is not necessarily applicable in a field that tries to question and change those norms and inequalities.

This chapter is a condensed version of additional research that Zoë Papaikonomou, one of the authors of this book, carried out in early 2021 in collaboration with Elodie Kona, researcher and research assistant for *The Inclusion Marathon.*[32] In the coming sections, we will take you through how our interviewees use scientific research in their daily work – also known as evidence-based work. We will explore what our interviewees define as 'evidence-based' within their field, how they practice evidence-based methods and the challenges they face as they do.

Definition of evidence-based work: a matter of perspective

Historical context is partly responsible for how theoretical frameworks and notions emerge in society, says American diversity practitioner Farzin Farzad. "Everyone has biases because the human brain recognizes and maintains patterns from the past. Similarly, science is not objective because knowledge comes from dominant ideologies and those in positions of power. This is also true within research institutions."

Scientific research is subject to the dominant normative perspectives from the colonial era. But what was once considered 'the truth' may no longer be relevant or valuable in today's day and age. Thus, the diversity practitioners we interviewed don't regard evidence-based research and practices as the silver bullet to solving society's inequalities.

Two questions linger from conversations with diversity practitioners about their perspective on evidence-based work: who determines what counts as 'evidence'? And what is the definition of the 'quality' of knowledge? These are issues that diversity practitioners face daily because the answers to these questions affect the extent to which there is room for diversity, equity and inclusion in the workplace.

What is quality?

Quality is sometimes seen as a measure that facilitates exclusion. The question here is: who decides what is or is not studied? Which interest groups decide or are allowed to participate?[33] The quality of research is related to how the research community looks at society. From what perspective is culture viewed? Hence, the quality of research is challenging to define.

A great example is evidence-based research within the medical community, where different stakeholders often influence 'quality' and conflicts of interest arise. In those instances, evidence that does not correspond to the desired results may never see the light of day.

Sociologist Willem Schinkel refers to social science research's neocolonial knowledge production. Theoretical concepts for analysis are fixed in advance and based on biases from the dominant group.[34] He criticizes evidence-based work that is considered high-quality while excluding all other perspectives. Willem Schinkel states that the lack of diversity (of thought) within knowledge institutions, such as universities, leads to a lack of quality information and knowledge.

In conclusion, whether research is high in quality or not is difficult to define. Daily routine indicates which aspects of scientific research are applicable in the workplace. Nevertheless, diversity practitioners describe evidence-based work mainly as carrying out their daily activities based on qualitative and quantitative research data. In this process, research is the starting point for creating 'best practices' in the workplace and vice versa.

Practice-oriented evidence

The diversity practitioner must have an eye for the specific organizational context and have a practice-oriented approach. There is a need to help shape scientific developments from practice to close the perceived gap between scientific knowledge and practice. Diversity practitioners emphasize the importance of being mindful of their work's specific context. They often build their theoretical framework in the workplace and company environments.

As part of an evidence-based approach, diversity practitioners often exchange information. Collecting and comparing personal experiences from different situations and various organizations are also considered evidence-based. Additionally, having an eye for different perspectives touches on intersectional thinking, which we discussed in more detail in our chapter *Definitions*. Researcher Nancy Jouwe summarizes intersectionality as how our various identities affect one another "at the material, institutional and symbolic levels, and face discrimination or positions of power differently at these levels."[35]

The diversity practitioners we interviewed actively seek to close the researcher-practitioner gap by, for example, partnering with universities to contribute to research through a practical lens.[36] Further, diversity practitioners monitor their interventions and test them against real-world situations. It is a continuous learning process.

Practice: how do diversity practitioners put 'evidence-based' into practice?

The usefulness of evidence depends on an organization's identity and corporate culture. Terence Guiamo, former Head of Diversity and Inclusion at PwC Netherlands, explains that a data-driven approach within PwC stems from its origins as an accounting firm: "Accountants are very much into numbers and data. If you don't substantiate diversity numerically, it is more difficult to get people on board."

How diversity practitioners put evidence-based research into practice varies by level within the organization. Bettina Haarbosch, Program Manager of Diversity & Inclusion at the Dutch Railways (NS), notices that top management often yearns for research and facts to inform their decisions. She is not alone. According to several diversity practitioners, top management attaches great importance to scientific evidence based on facts and numbers.

Our interviewees also consider using unbiased researchers to check which methods do not work as evidence-based practices within companies. Scientists from outside the organization are brought in to gather evidence concerning an issue within the organization.

Diversity practitioners also exchange information, (good) practices and experiences to determine which studies serve as relevant evidence within their field. As a result, (good) practices from other organizations and experiences from colleagues are also included as part of evidence-based work.

Diversity and inclusion are about empathy and emotion. Several diversity practitioners mention the importance of feelings and emotions as evidence. The interviewees indicated that 'touching people' helps raise awareness about diversity, equity and inclusion, thus stimulating action. This methodology could qualify as qualitative research, but it often goes far beyond interviews or focus groups. Our interviewees start with (personal) experiences, stories and conversations to create an evidence-based approach. Diversity practitioner Gatra Peshtaz uses storytelling to spark emotions in people. "I always start with my story and try to link other stories to mine and each other. I expose that the patterns and structures of stories are quite similar in everyone's experience."

"Inclusion is about people, and that includes feelings. I like to work with human evidence": Hanan Challouki, an expert in inclusive communication, likes to work with qualitative evidence, such as conversations and interviews. She believes an in-depth interview reveals much more about the workplace atmosphere than surveys with percentages and numbers.

Challenges: what makes evidence-based work difficult?

Diversity practitioners believe that we need to be mindful of the history and context in which knowledge has been produced. DEI advisor Jeftha Pattikawa notes that because of historical inequality in science, there is still a dynamic nowadays in which certain forms of knowledge are not given space to exist.

Because all kinds of prejudices and stereotypes occur within organizations, diversity practitioners say it is crucial to be aware of exclusionary mechanisms in research. This is also about power. Who determines what is researched and how is evidence-based work carried out and interpreted? The question remains: What kind of knowledge is considered legitimate? Jeftha Pattikawa sums it up sharply: "You can't use the same methodologies and knowledge to change something if they support exclusion."

History shows that science has not been adequately inclusive and diverse. Diversity practitioners point out that outdated ideas and theories are often built upon evidence-based research. They also state that while much research has been done on diversity, equity and inclusion, it's been more from an American context, which is not always applicable to the Dutch situation. When tackling DEI in the Netherlands, looking at what Dutch literature offers is essential.

Marten Bos notes that bicultural and Black researchers are quickly seen as activists or politically driven. Yet, they have been publishing studies on diversity, equity and inclusion in the Netherlands for years. Take a look at renowned researchers Gloria Wekker and Philomena Essed, whose work has caused a stir in the Netherlands and who are more likely to be labeled as activists in the public debate (as if being an activist were a bad thing).

Another mismatch our interviewees mention is that most general DEI research is often seen as too broad and not applicable for organizations' specific contexts. Furthermore, diversity practitioners indicate that the research methods are not always sufficiently aligned with practice. They experience a heavy emphasis on quantitative and KPI-driven (KPI = Key Performance Indicator) processes, while they should actually consider people and their feelings, rather than just statistics.

Data never stands alone. It remains important to realize that data would not exist without the people behind it. The human aspect must remain the focal point in evidence-based work. Laura Cominencia, HR change manager, recalls situations where administrators concluded that everything was going well based on the numbers while the reality on the shop floor sometimes showed an entirely different story.

So within HR – as in any environment – we must consider people's prejudices. Laura Cominencia explains that research results are interpreted based on the researcher's assumptions, influences and background. "We have to be careful when considering interpretations as the truth. If a group of similar or like-minded individuals interprets the data, the results may be biased."

Jean-Paul Lucassen, People Analytics Lead at Dutch Railways (NS), believes collaboration and alignment between practice and research are important, especially in a world driven by numbers. "It is important to keep looking at how theory and practice can complement each other."

In conclusion

Diversity practitioners are critical of existing theories from a white, male, heteronormative, upperclass perspective and seek evidence from other (marginalized) perspectives to supplement their knowledge. Some examples of research that fit this description are the work of Gloria Wekker, Philomena Essed, Sara Ahmed, Audre Lorde, Edward Said and Sinan Çankaya.

Scientific research and experiences are used to propose and implement processes and interventions to increase diversity, equity and inclusion. But diversity practitioners also use research to legitimize their work; in their experience, top management often requests thorough examinations. An evidence-based approach then helps to substantiate the proposed plans and increases the power of persuasion.

However, in practice, it turns out that diversity issues cannot always be properly answered based on scientific research. The extent to which research is helpful for the specific challenges diversity practitioners face in practice differs by context. Consequently, diversity practitioners share evidence-based practices alongside science and try to fill in the gaps with personal and professional experiences.

Scientific research can help diversity practitioners introduce interventions and processes within organizations. Diversity practitioners play an important role in interacting and developing the available science and best practices for the DEI field. They consciously select the most appropriate approach, and they adapt it to the specific context they are dealing with.

Science and research are not objective and often biased, especially within the DEI field. Scientific knowledge alone is not enough to increase diversity, equity and inclusion in organizations.

Evidence-based work requires a (self-)critical attitude and is an ongoing (learning) process. As a result, we repeat the words of feminist writer and poet Audre Lorde: "For the master's tools will never dismantle the master's house. They may allow us temporarily to beat him at his own game, but they will never enable us to bring about genuine change."[37]

Tips for Employees

Moving toward a diverse, inclusive and equitable workplace is a complex change issue in an organization and should not be any individual employee's responsibility. Employees who experience exclusion should especially not carry this burden. Yet, those who are excluded notice when a work environment is unsafe and could offer insights into how an organization could become more inclusive. This book provides tools to change organizations and support those who experience discrimination in the workplace.

We divided the tips into general recommendations for a safe work environment that everyone can contribute to and specific advice for those experiencing exclusion.

General advice

- Be yourself, but don't believe your lifestyle is better than someone else's.
- The same goes for all kinds of different communication styles. One way of communicating is not better than the other.
- We bond more easily with people we feel connected to because of similarities and resemblances. Be aware of this inclination towards what's similar and approach colleagues who you don't feel familiar with immediately.
- Everyone has prejudices and assumptions. Once you can accept and examine your biases, you can make changes.
- An inclusive workplace is a shared responsibility. Be aware of the fact that the *emotional labor* can be more intense for employees who belong to a (marginalized) minority:
  - Don't only ask people who experience exclusion for advice on what to do. Consider actions to counteract exclusion and discuss these suggestions with those affected.

- Consider whether you should ask them directly about their background (e.g., religious or cultural) or whether you should find out for yourself.
- Discomfort and vulnerability can deepen a relationship with a colleague; don't shy away from it. But don't use it as an excuse to centralize your own discomfort.
- Be concerned for the safety of others. Speak up about discriminatory jokes or actions, bullying and subtle exclusion in the workplace.

Advice for employees who experience (subtle) exclusion

- Find peers: look for colleagues who share your experiences to exchange frustrations and successes and to feel less lonely. In other words, find or create a safe space for yourself.
- Find allies, colleagues who share the same mission and support you.
- State your boundaries:
  - Sharing your experience with exclusion/discrimination may make your colleagues more aware of these experiences, but you are not obligated to do so (every time). Professional organizations are dedicated to raising awareness, and trained experts can use their experiences to spread awareness effectively.
  - It's completely fine not to want to take part in the discussion at all times. Creating awareness of discrimination and exclusion takes a lot of energy. There is nothing wrong with picking your battles.
  - Not every joke is funny; some jokes are discriminatory. Be an ally when the joke concerns a colleague, even though the comments don't directly affect you or don't concern you specifically at that time.
  - When conversations about diversity, equity and inclusion occur, don't be afraid to point out that you are not 'the subject' but an equal partner in the conversation.

- Being part of a marginalized group, you are usually more used to compensating for other people's discomfort (about your ethnicity, disability, gender identity, etc.). You don't have to do this. Some advice on how to not take on the other person's discomfort:
  · When someone asks you an uncomfortable question, repeat that question.
  · State that you don't like a comment.
  · You don't always have to respond immediately. It may help to get back to it another time.

Biographies of interviewees

The interviews for this book took place between 2020 and 2021 and these biographies are drawn from that period. Current employers or employment may have changed.

Siham Achahboun is the Program Manager of Cultural Diversity and Inclusion at insurer Achmea. She is also the founder and president of the Rising Ummah Foundation, an organization dedicated to strengthening the position of Muslims with physical disabilities within the community.

Siham Ammal is a consultant and trainer on Diversity and Inclusion at *Leeuwendaal* consultancy, where she specializes in inclusive talent management. She gives training courses on inclusive recruitment and selection to a variety of clients.

Siela Ardjosemito-Jethoe is Diversity & Inclusion Officer at the *Hogeschool der Kunsten* in The Hague. She also runs her own company Connecting the Dots unlimited to provide training, coaching and advice to the welfare, education and cultural sectors.

Carel Boers is a coach and leadership development consultant and founded *De Integere Overheid* with Fatima Elatik to guide professionals within public sector organizations.

Marten Bos is a freelance trainer, speaker, coach, supervisor and author on diversity and inclusion. He developed 'diversity cards' to capture layered identities and also strongly believes in the intersectional approach within DEI.

Karima el Bouchtaoui is the Director of Ocullus Consultancy, an agency that helps organizations with their diversity policies. She started as a policy officer within the municipality of The Hague; as time passed, her positions became more DEI-oriented.

Kaveh Bouteh is a consultant and trainer at Pharos, Center of Expertise on Health Disparities. He organizes sessions to create an inclusive organizational culture and develops tools for transformative leadership.

Danielle Braun is an organizational anthropologist and expert in organizational culture and leadership. She is also the Director of the Academy for Organizational Culture, a platform for corporate anthropology in the Netherlands.

Marieke van den Brink is Professor of Gender and Diversity at Radboud University Nijmegen. She has been working on several research projects on gender, diversity and inclusion.

Saniye Çelik is a college professor specialized in diversity issues at *Hogeschool Leiden* and teaches the course 'Inclusive leadership for public leaders & administrators'. She leads several studies on diversity issues within public sector organizations, including in education, municipalities, central government and the police.

Hanan Challouki is the founder of Inclusified, a company focused on inclusive strategies and campaigns. In 2018, she obtained a spot on the Forbes 30 Under 30 list for her innovative methods. She also produces the podcast *Wat Zij Wil* (in English: What She Wants) to encourage ambitious women to pursue their entrepreneurial dreams.

Laura Cominencia is an independent HR consultant specializing in diversity and inclusion and has been working in HR for fifteen years. Currently, she is Senior HR Advisor at the municipality of Rotterdam.

Ismahan Çürük is an expert in learning and development. She is the co-owner of Bureau Vie, which trains, coaches and advises organizations to work more inclusively.

Marianne Dijkshoorn is a consultant and speaker on accessibility and inclusion. She focuses on making events more accessible for people with disabilities. She also wrote a book on this subject with guidelines for event organizers.

Fatima Elatik has years of experience in the governmental and political industry and is the co-founder of *De Integere Overheid* initiative. With her consultancy firm, Elatik Consultancy, she coaches professionals on leadership, diversity management and the balance between government interests and the business world.

Astrid Elburg is a consultant and advises on strategy, transformation and ethics. She also develops training courses on resilience against exclusion and racism.

Martin van Engel is a Diversity and Inclusion Advisor committed to making culturally diverse cultural expressions more visible. He is a member of the Dutch Unesco Commission and Amsterdam Arts Council.

Farzin Farzad is an American diversity practitioner focusing on power relations within organizations. Recently, he started his consulting firm, Critical Equity Consulting, with which he guides organizations toward more equity in the workplace.

Halleh Ghorashi was appointed Professor of Diversity and Integration at VU University Amsterdam in 2012. This professor of Diversity has a background in social sciences and anthropology. Her work and research on the lives of migrants and refugees take on different perspectives.

Terence Guiamo is the Global Director of Inclusion, Diversity and Belonging at Just Eat Takeaway.com. He was Chairman at Agora Network, a Dutch network dedicated to increasing cultural diversity within all layers of organizations.

Bettina Haarbosch has worked at the Dutch Railways (Nederlandse Spoorwegen) since 2006 and as Program Manager of Diversity and Inclusion since 2016, focusing on senior management.

Machteld de Jong is a lecturer on Diversity at Hogeschool Inholland, conducts research, and publishes on equal opportunities in higher education and society.

Manuela Kalsky is a theologian and expert on religion and meaning in a multicultural and multifaith society. She is a Professor of Theology and Society at the *Vrije Universiteit Amsterdam*.

Machiel Keestra is a philosopher with specific knowledge of cognitive neuroscience. In addition to his job as Assistant Professor at the Faculty of Natural Sciences, Mathematics and Computer Science at the University of Amsterdam, he is also the diversity officer.

Joy Lodarmasse is Manager of Diversity and Inclusion at energy network company Alliander. As a Corporate Social Responsibility advisor, her task is to shape Alliander into a socially responsible and inclusive company.

Elsa van de Loo is a human rights lawyer and a trainer at The Netherlands Institute of Human Rights. She gives training on stereotyping and prejudice in the recruitment and selection process.

Jean-Paul Lucassen is the People Analytics Lead at Dutch Railways (NS), where he and his team gather fact-based insights to make HR processes more effective and improve decision-making.

Esther Mollema gives lectures and consults worldwide on successful business, high-performance organizations (HPOs) and leadership, inclusion, diversity and unconscious bias.

Geraldine Moodley is a human rights lawyer and mediator with experience in customer relations, project management, corporate social responsibility and more. She has worked as a CSR advisor, mediator and negotiator to governments, management and Boards, including as Director of Diversity, Equity and Inclusion at Nike Europe, Middle East and Africa.

Shervin Nekuee is the Senior Advisor on Diversity and Inclusion at the Ministry of Social Affairs and Employment. He is also an independent writer and columnist and has written a book, *The Persian Paradox: Stories from the Islamic Republic of Iran.*

Jeftha Pattikawa is the National Archive Inclusive Program Leader as part of the Ministry of Education, Culture and Science. He is also a Rotterdam Council for Arts and Culture council member.

Gatra Peshtaz is an anthropologist and speaker who has her own company to advise organizations on their diversity and inclusion strategy. She also works for the Dutch Refugee Council as an employment consultant.

Nicole Reimink-Böttger is Product Owner, Diversity and Inclusion at ABN AMRO Bank. She organizes mentoring programs and is the D&I point of contact for all employees within the bank.

Shiva Roofeh is a curious rebel working in leadership development and learning design with the lenses of equity, justice and power-sharing. She is a secret punk and perpetual smiler with experience in higher education and the corporate sector.

Lucho Rubio Repáraz is a sociologist, socio-intercultural mediator. Since 2012 he has been a lecturer at the Faculty of Social Work of the Hogeschool Leiden on diversity, sociology and ethics.

Onur Şahin is pursuing his Ph.D. in research into the relationship between "being different" and inclusion in the workplace at Utrecht University at the Faculty of Social Sciences. He is interested in the factors that contribute to a more inclusive workplace.

Bouchra Talidi has her own organizational consulting firm Inclusioncy. With her team, she coaches organizations with (leadership) training and change management.

Joan Tol is the Project Manager of Equal Opportunities, Diversity and Inclusion at the MBO Council (Council for Education in the Netherlands). She specializes in behavioral change, and her approach is mainly in change management.

Mary Tupan-Wenno is Executive Director at ECHO, an expertise center for diversity policy. She has more than thirty years of experience with issues of diversity and inclusion in education and the labor market, with a specific focus on ethnic diversity.

Melek Usta is the founder and director of the recruitment, selection and consulting agency, Colorful People. She is also a member of several advisory boards, including those of Hogeschool van Amsterdam and Volksbank, and a member of the Amsterdam Economic Board.

Mohan Verstegen is a Policy Advisor and doctor at the Dutch Department of Defense and is also committed to diversity and inclusion within the Department of Defense. He is also very active on various social media platforms to draw attention to diversity and inclusion.

Nezahat Yildirim is Senior Recruiter/Advisor Diversity and Inclusion at the central government. She has a recruitment and selection agency, Business Recruitment Services & Consultancy, to advise highly educated multicultural candidates.

Acknowledgements

We thank our interviewees, the many diversity practitioners and researchers without whom this book wouldn't exist. We gratefully merged their experiences, knowledge and sharp analyses into one. Your trust and commitment were insightful and heartwarming.

We are deeply indebted to our 'committee of the wise', who provided critical and constructive feedback to our words: Sahar Noor, Vivian Acquah, Hinde Chergui, Rocher Koendjbiharie, Şeydâ Buurman-Kutsal, Emma Veldhuizen and Onno Halsema.

Our book would have been published much later without the help of our editorial assistant Elodie Kona. Elodie, you are a book-saver; thank you for your skillful work and commitment. We also thank Lisanne Groothuis, Anouk Torbeyns and Elodie Harreman for their help in editing the interviews.

Lotte Akkerman ably addressed our textual and stylistic matters in the original Dutch version of our book. We also thank our coordinating editor Jaap Wagenaar from publisher Amsterdam University Press and external editor Yulia Knol. We especially thank acquiring publisher Inge van der Bijl for believing in our book.

For bringing about this extensive summary of *The Inclusion Marathon* in English, we are greatly indebted to Elodie Kona, not only for aptly summarizing our work but also translating it. We also thank DEI experts Shiva Roofeh and Farzin Farzad from the bottoms of our hearts for their insightful feedback on the summary, inspiring conversations on its content and especially for their awesome preface. We would also like to thank our text editor Elyzabeth Gorman for her sharp eye and continuous warm involvement.

A warm shout-out also goes to those who raise issues of power abuse and discrimination every day. We thank those who take to the barricades, either online or offline, each in their unique way. We're grateful for those on the frontlines now, before and in the future.

I, Kauthar, don't know where to start. I have a lot to say, but not everything can be put into words.

I'm grateful to be part of a movement fighting for equity. So many people are committed to the fight; sometimes they are visible, but often they are not. And they keep going anyway. It's so heartwarming.

I'm grateful for all who came before us, those who, more often than not, paid a high price. They kept believing in what they stood for. 'Still I rise' is part of the legacy they left us. It is so valuable.

I have a lot of gratitude for those who reach out when I fall, those who laugh with me when we knock the dust off and those who are willing to hold up the mirror, even when it's ugly.

I feel blessed with the people in my life, those staying and growing with me. In your reflection, I see the power of our shared vulnerability. Thank you so much.

I, Zoë, thank my family and friends for their unconditional love and patience. Without your ongoing interest, help and sound advice, this book wouldn't have been finished. Dear Jamie, Mila, Jurre and Mom, you are the lights of my life and the ground on which I thrive.

I also thank the unique network I have built over the past years in the field of diversity, equity and inclusion – offline and online. You inspire me daily; I learn every day. Thank you for your unbridled dedication and critical feedback.

Special thanks to my friend Annebregt Dijkman, with whom I wrote my first book, One'sy Muller & Vinny Tailor, my podcast partners in crime, and Ibtisam Harrak, for our mutual trust, support and space to make mistakes and learn from them. I'm also grateful for the insightful and warm conversations with Usha Marhé.

Finally, I'd like to thank my former and current colleagues at the online platform *Nieuw Wij*. For the past few years, they've allowed me to freely research power and discomfort, particularly complex and incredibly uncomfortable topics. Thank you for the critical exchange and support in tackling these subjects my way.

*"Our lives begin to end the day we become
silent about things that matter."*
– Martin Luther King Jr.

Kauthar Bouchallikht and Zoë Papaikonomou, July 2021/December 2022 (English summary)

Notes

1. Ahmed, Sara. *Living a Feminist Life* (Durham: Duke University Press, 2017).
2. Papaikonomou, Zoë. "Inclusief de crisis door?" ["Going Through the Crisis Inclusively?"]. *Nieuw Wij*, April 1, 2020.
3. Gassam Asare, Janice. "Companies: Now Is Not The Time To Put Diversity And Inclusion On The Back Burner." *Forbes*, April 5, 2020.
4. Study on inequality during the COVID-19 pandemic: McKinsey & Company. (2020). *Black Americans Face Disproportionate Share of Disruption from Coronavirus*. Other relevant studies listed under References at the end of this summary are Garcia e.a. (2021), Sabatello e.a. (2021), Hanage e.a. (2020), Ruprecht e.a. (2020) and Chatters e.a. (2020).
5. More on the Black Lives Matter Movement in Dutch: https://nos.nl/op3/artikel/2336375-dit-is-het-verhaal-achter-de-black-lives-matter-beweging; https://nl.wikipedia.org/wiki/Black_Lives_Matter.
6. Papaikonomou, Zoë. "Aminata Cairo: Via het Zwarte verhaal gaat het over ons allemaal" ["The Story of Black People Affects Us All"]. *Nieuw Wij*, September 29, 2020.
7. Ahmed, Sara. *On Being Included: Racism and Diversity in Institutional Life*. (Durham: Duke University Press, 2012).
8. *Happy talk* is a concept coined by Sara Ahmed in her book *On Being Included: Racism and Diversity in Institutional Life* (Durham: Duke University Press, 2012).
9. Several studies show that diversity brings many benefits, including better financial performance, including *Why Diversity Matters*. McKinsey & Company (2015). Other studies show that diverse teams only work if they are well-managed, including Hydari (2021) Shemla e.a. (2019) listed under References at the end of this summary.
10. More on personal pronouns in Dutch sources: https://www.transgenderinfo.nl/wp/wp-content/uploads/2020/10/gender-neutrale-voornaamwoorden-in-het-nederlands.pdf. Associated Press describes the capital letter as a recognition of the identity of minority groups. As such, they are seen as people, not a color:
11. https://apnews.com/article/archive-race-and-ethnicity-9105661462.

12. For more on inclusive writing: Samuel, Mounir. *Handreiking Waarden voor een nieuwe taal* [*Handbook on Values for a New Language*] (Amsterdam: Code Diversiteit & Inclusie, 2021) and the National Museum of World Cultures' guide: *Woorden doen ertoe: Een incomplete gids voor woordkeuze binnen de culturele sector* [*Words Matter: An Incomplete Guide for Word Choice Within the Cultural Sector*] (Amsterdam, etc.: NMVW, 2018).

13. Papaikonomou, Zoë and Annebregt Dijkman. *"Heb je een boze moslim voor mij?" Over inclusieve journalistiek* [*"Got an Angry Muslim for me?" On Inclusive Journalism*]. (Amsterdam: Amsterdam University Press, 2018). A collection of Zoë's interviews and articles can be found on this website: https://www.nieuwwij.nl/personen/zoe-papaikonomou/.

14. For more info on equity in the international context, please see: https://www.ywboston.org/2019/03/beyond-the-acronym-dei/ & https://medium.com/the-ascent/why-d-i-doesn't-work-without-the-e-740cc95af561.

15. Amnesty International on equality and equal treatment (in Dutch): https://www.amnesty.nl/encyclopedie/gelijkheid-en-gelijke-behandeling.

16. Papaikonomou, Zoë. "Philomena Essed: uit elke ongemak komt een verrassende ontdekking voort" ["Philomena Essed: out of every discomfort comes a surprising discovery"]. *Nieuw Wij*, March 20, 2020.

17. Papaikonomou, Zoë. "Privilege betekent niet dat alles makkelijk is, wel meer kans op wind mee" ["Privilege Does Not Make Everything Easy, but It Does Mean That There Is More Chance of Tailwind"]. *Nieuw Wij*, August 6, 2020.

18. Crenshaw, Kimberlé. *Demarginalizing the Intersection of Race and Sex: A Black Feminist Critique of Antidiscrimination Doctrine, Feminist Theory and Antiracist Politics* (University of Chigaco Legal Forum, 1989).

19. Wekker, Gloria. *Witte onschuld: Paradoxen van kolonialisme en ras.* [White Innocence: Paradoxes of Colonialism and Race]. (Amsterdam: Amsterdam University Press, 2018).

20. For more on Kick Out Zwarte Piet (KOZP) [Kick Out Black Pete], see: https://kozwartepiet.nl/ & https://nl.wikipedia.org/wiki/Kick_Out_Zwarte_Piet

21. Challouki, Hanan. *Inclusieve communicatie* [*Inclusive Communication*]. (Kalmthout: Uitgeverij Pelckmans, 2021)

22. Papaikonomou, Zoë. "Het is belangrijk dat er rolmodellen zijn in alle lagen van de organisatie" ["It's Important to Have Role Models at all Levels of the Organization"]. *Nieuw Wij,* June 27, 2019.

23. More information on emotional labor, see: Suico, Theresa. "Emotional Labor and Women of Color in the Workplace: A Reality Check". *The City of Portland.* https://www.portlandoregon.gov/article/686010.

24. Papaikonomou, Zoë and Dijkman, Annebregt. *"Heb je een boze moslim voor mij?" Over inclusieve journalistiek* [*"Got an Angry Muslim for me?" On Inclusive Journalism*]. (Amsterdam: Amsterdam University Press, 2018), p. 123.

25. Lorde, Audre. *Sister Outsider: Essays and speeches.* (Trumansburg: Crossing Press, 1984).

26. Halleh Ghorashi discusses the 'in-between spaces" in this interview with *Zorg+Welzijn* (Dutch): https://www.zorgwelzijn.nl/exclusie-is-natuurlijker-dan-inclusie/.

27. Ahmed, Sara. *On Being Included: Racism and Diversity in Institutional Life.* (Durham: Duke University Press, 2012) p.141-173.

28. Joan Tol uses the ADKAR model (*Awareness, Desire, Knowledge, Ability and Reinforcement*). This model starts from the idea that change originates from the individual in the organization. It was developed by Jeff Hiatt and introduced into practice by Prosci, a recognized change management consulting and training firm. The ADKAR model is primarily intended as a coaching tool to help and assist employees during change processes within organizations. https://www.toolshero.nl/verandermanagement/adkar-model-hiatt/ & https://www.prosci.com/methodology/adkar. Jeff Hiatt wrote a book on the ADKAR model: Hiatt, Jeff. *ADKAR, A model for change in business, government and our community.* (Fort Collins: Prosci Learning Center Publications, 2006).

29. Ahmed, Sara. *Living a Feminist Life.* (Durham: Duke University Press, 2017). Find out more at https://feministkilljoys.com/.

30. Meyerson, Debra E. *Tempered Radicals: How People Use Difference to Inspire Change at Work.* (New York: Two Rivers Distribution, 2003).

31. This division of roles is based our interviews with a special thanks to college professor Saniye Çelik.

32. Kona, Elodie and Papaikonomou, Zoë. *Kennis is macht: Hoe kan evidencebased werken bijdragen aan een meer diverse, inclusieve*

en gelijkwaardige werkvloer? [*Knowledge is Power: How Can Evidence-Based Work Contribute to a More Diverse, Inclusive and Equal Workplace?*]. (Diversity Media, 2021).

33. Greenhalgh e.a. "Evidence-Based Medicine: a Movement in Crisis?" (*The BMJ*, 2014).

34. Schinkel, Willem. "Against 'Immigrant Integration': for an End to Neocolonial Knowledge Production" (*Comparative Migration Studies,* 2018), p. 1-17.

35. Nancy Jouwe in: Witte, Robert. "Intersectionaliteit, wat moeten we ermee?" ["Intersectionality, what should we do with it?"]. (February 25, 2019).

36. As described in: Tenhiälä, Aino e.a., "The Research-Practice Gap in Human Resource Management: A Cross-Cultural Study", (*Human Resource Management* 55, 2016). P 179-200 and DeNisi, S.A. e.a., "Research and practice in HRM: A historical perspective"'. (*Human Resource Management Review* 24, 2014), p. 219-231.

37. Lorde, Audre. *Master's Tools Will Never Dismantle The Master's House* (Penguin Modern Classics Series: 23 Reissue). (London: Penguin Classics, 2021).

References

Ahmed, Sara. *On Being Included: Racism and Diversity in Institutional Life*. (Durham: Duke University Press, 2012).

Ahmed, Sara. *Living a Feminist Life*. (Durham: Duke University Press, 2017).

Asare, Janice Gassam."Companies: Now Is Not The Time To Put Diversity And Inclusion On The Back Burner", *Forbes*, April 5, 2020.

Challouki, Hanan. *Inclusieve communicatie [Inclusive Communication]*. (Kalmthout: Pelckmans Uitgevers, 2021).

Chatters, L.M., Taylor, H.O., & Taylor, R.J. "Older Black Americans During COVID-19: Race and Age Double Jeopardy", *Health Education & Behavior, 47*(6) (2020) p. 855-860.

Crenshaw, Kimberlé (1989) *Demarginalizing the Intersection of Race and Sex: A Black Feminist Critique of Antidiscrimination Doctrine, Feminist Theory and Antiracist Politics* (University of Chigaco Legal Forum, 1989).

DeNisi, A.S., Wilson, M.S., & Biteman, J. "Research and practice in HRM: A historical perspective", *Human Resource Management Review, 24*(3) (2014) p. 219-231.

Garcia, M.A., Homan, P.A., García, C., & Brown, T.H. "The Color of COVID-19: Structural Racism and the Disproportionate Impact of the Pandemic on Older Black and Latinx Adults", *The Journals of Gerontology. Series B, Psychological Sciences and Social Sciences, 76*(3), (2021).

Greenhalgh, T., Howick, J., & Maskrey, N. "Evidence-Based Medicine: a Movement in Crisis?", *BMJ: British Medical Journal*, 348 (2014).

Hanage, W.P., Testa, C., Chen, J. T., Davis, L., Pechter, E., Seminario, P., Santillana, M., & Krieger, N. "COVID-19: US Federal Accountability for Entry, Spread, and Inequities-Lessons for the Future", *European Journal of Epidemiology, 35*(11), (2020) p. 995-1006.

Hiatt, Jeff. *ADKAR: A model for change in business, government and our community*. (Fort Collins: Prosci Learning Center Publications, 2006).

Hunt, Vivianne, Layton, Dennis & Prince, Sara. *Why Diversity Matters*. (McKinsey & Company, 2015).

Hydari, Sabah Alam. *Countering otherness: Fostering Integration Within Teams*. (McKinsey & Company, 2021).

Kalas, Ivana & Lange, Tesseltje de. "Liever zelfstandig dan gediscrimineerd op de werkvloer" ["Rather self-employed than discriminated against in the workplace"], *Website Radboud Universiteit*, March 23, 2020.

Kona, Elodie and Papaikonomou, Zoë. *Kennis is macht: Hoe kan evidencebased werken bijdragen aan een meer diverse, inclusieve en gelijkwaardige werkvloer? [Knowledge is Power: How Can Evidence-Based Work Contribute to a More Diverse, Inclusive and Equal Workplace?]*. (Amsterdam: Diversity Media, 2021).

Lorde, Audre. *Sister Outsider. Essays and speeches.* (Trumansburg: Crossing Press, 1984).

McKinsey & Company. *Black Americans Face Disproportionate Share of Disruption from Coronavirus*. (2020).

Meyerson, D.E. *Tempered Radicals: How People Use Difference to Inspire Change at Work*. (New York: Two Rivers Distribution, 2003).

Nationaal Museum van Wereldculturen. *Woorden doen ertoe: Een incomplete gids voor woordkeuze binnen de culturele sector* [*Words Matter: An Incomplete Guide for Word Choice Within the Cultural Sector*]. (Amsterdam, etc.: NMVW, 2018).

Papaikonomou, Zoë. "Het is belangrijk dat er rolmodellen zijn in alle lagen van de organisatie" ["It's Important to Have Role Models at all Levels of the Organization"], *Nieuw Wij*, June 27, 2019.

Papaikonomou, Zoë. "Inclusief de crisis door?" ["Going Through the Crisis Inclusively?"], *Nieuw Wij*, April 1, 2020.

Papaikonomou, Zoë. "'Via het Zwarte verhaal gaat het over ons allemaal': Aminata Cairo wil waardering teweegbrengen voor mensen en hun verhalen' ["The Story of Black People Affects Us All"], *Nieuw Wij*, September 29, 2020.

Papaikonomou, Zoë. "Privilege betekent niet dat alles makkelijk is, wel meer kans op wind mee" ["Privilege Does Not Make Everything Easy, but It Does Mean That There Is More Chance of Tailwind"], *Nieuw Wij*, December 19, 2019.

Papaikonomou, Zoë. "Philomena Essed: uit elke ongemak komt een verrassende ontdekking voort" ["Philomena Essed: out of every discomfort comes a surprising discovery"], *Nieuw Wij*, March 20, 2020.

Papaikonomou, Zoë and Dijkman, Annebregt. *"Heb je een boze moslim voor mij?" Over inclusieve journalistiek.* [*"Got an Angry Muslim for me?" On Inclusive Journalism*]. (Amsterdam: Amsterdam University Press, 2018).

Ruprecht, M.M., Wang, X., Johnson, A.K., Xu, J., Felt, D., Ihenacho, S., Stonehouse, P., Curry, C.W., DeBroux, C., Costa, D., & Phillips II, G. "Evidence of Social and Structural COVID-19 Disparities by Sexual Orientation, Gender Identity, and Race/Ethnicity in an Urban Environment", *Journal of Urban Health*, 98(1), (2020) p. 27-40.

Sabatello, M., Jackson Scroggins, M., Goto, G., Santiago, A., McCormick, A., Morris, K.J., Daulton, C.R., Easter, C.L., & Darien, G. "Structural Racism in the COVID-19 Pandemic: Moving Forward", *American Journal of Bioethics*, 21(3), (2021) p. 56-74.

Samuel, Mounir. *Handreiking waarden voor een nieuwe taal.* [*Handbook on Values for a New Language*]. (Amsterdam: Code Diversiteit & Inclusie, 2021).

Schinkel, Willem. "Against 'immigrant integration': for an end to neocolonial knowledge production", *Comparative Migration Studies*, 6(1), (2018) p. 1-17.

Schoenmakers, Demi. "Waarom het heel belangrijk is dat je opkomt voor je collega's" ["Why it is very important to stand up for your colleagues"], *Carrière. nu*, May 7, 2019.

Shemla, Meir and Wegge, Jürgen. "Managing diverse teams by enhancing team identification: The mediating role of perceived diversity", *Human Relations (New York)*, 72(4), (2019) p. 755-777.

Suico, Theresa. (z.d.). "Emotional Labor and Women of Color in the Workplace: A Reality Check", City of Portland.

Tenhiälä, A., Giluk, T.L., Kepes, S., Simón, C., Oh, I., & Kim, S. "The Research-Practice Gap in Human Resource Management: A Cross-Cultural Study", *Human Resource Management*, 55(2), (2016) p. 179-200.

Wekker, Gloria. *Witte onschuld: Paradoxen van kolonialisme en ras*. [*White Innocence: Paradoxes of Colonialism and Race*]. (Amsterdam: Amsterdam University Press, 2018).

Witte, Robert. "Intersectionaliteit, wat moeten we ermee?" ["Intersectionality, what should we do with it?"], *Utrecht: Movisie*, February 25, 2019.

Internet sources

https://apnews.com/article/archive-race-and-ethnicity-9105661462
https://feministkilljoys.com/
https://kozwartepiet.nl/
https://medium.com/the-ascent/why-d-i-doesnt-work-without-the-e-740cc95af561
https://nl.wikipedia.org/wiki/Kick_Out_Zwarte_Piet
https://www.amnesty.nl/encyclopedie/gelijkheid-en-gelijke-behandeling
https://www.cvc.nl
https://www.icm.nl/opleidingen-en-trainingen/persoonlijke-effectiviteit/
    conflicthantering/
https://www.portlandoregon.gov/article/686010
https://www.prosci.com/methodology/adkar
https://www.seyda.nl/omgaan-met-weerstand/
https://www.toolshero.nl/verandermanagement/adkar-model-hiatt/
https://www.transgenderinfo.nl/wp/wp-content/uploads/2020/10/genderneutrale-
    voornaamwoorden-in-het-nederlands.pdf.
https://www.ywboston.org/2019/03/beyond-the-acronym-dei/
https://www.zorgwelzijn.nl/exclusie-is-natuurlijker-dan-inclusie/

Recommended literature for more in-depth study

Below, we have tried to make a broad selection of relevant (scientific) literature for those who want to delve deeper into the world of diversity, equity and inclusion. You will find our selection and literature tips from our interviewees in this list. We've also provided a selection from our interviewees' publications.

This list is not complete of course, but we hope it can be a run-up to further exploration.

Definitions

Ahmed, Sara. *Queer Phenomenology: Orientations, Objects, Others.* (Durham: Duke University Press, 2006).

Banaji, M.R., & Greenwald, A.G. *Blindspot: Hidden Biases of Good People.* (New York: Penguin Random House, 2016).

Braun, Danielle. *Da's gek: Een antropologische kijk op 'normaal'.* [That's crazy: An Anthropological View of What's Considered "Normal"]. (Amsterdam: Uitgeverij Water, 2018).

Çelik Saniye. *Diversiteit, de gewoonste zaak van de wereld?.* [*Diversity, The Most Common Thing in the World*]. (Leiden: Hogeschool Leiden, 2018).

Eberhardt, Jennifer L. *Biased.* (New York: Penguin Putnam Inc., 2019).

Ghorashi, Halleh. *Culturele diversiteit, Nederlandse identiteit en democratisch burgerschap.* [*Cultural diversity, Dutch Identity and Democratic Citizenship*]. (Den Haag: Sdu., 2010).

Hagendoorn, Louk N., & Nekuee, Shervin. *Education and Racism: A Cross National Inventory of Positive Effects of Education on Ethnic Tolerance.* (London: Routledge, 1999).

Jong, Machteld. de. *Diversiteit in het hoger onderwijs.* [*Diversity in the Higher Education System*]. Groningen: Noordhoff, 2014).

Kalsky Manuela. *Alsof ik thuis ben: Samenleven in een land vol verschillen.* [*Like Being at Home: Living Together in a Country Full of Differences*]. (Almere: Parthenon, 2013).

Page, Scott E. *Diversity and Complexity.* (Princeton: Princeton University Press, 2010)

Rothstein, Richard. *The Color of Law.* (New York: Liveright Publishing, 2017).

Society

Ahmed, Sara. *Strange Encounters: Embodied Others in Post-Coloniality.* (London: Taylor & Francis, 2013).

Ahmed, Sara. *Living a Feminist Life.* (Amsterdam: Amsterdam University Press, 2017).

Bouteldja, Houria. *Witte mensen, Joden en wij.* [*White People, Jews and Us*] (Amsterdam: Editie Leesmagazijn, 2020).

Brandsma, Bart. *Polarisatie: Inzicht in de dynamiek van wij-zij denken.* [*Polarization: Understanding the Dynamics of Us-versus-them Thinking*]. (Amsterdam: Boom Uitgevers, 2020).

Chemaly, Soraya. *Rage Becomes Her.* (Londen: Simon & Schuster, 2018).

Coates, Ta-Nehisi. *Between the World and Me.* (New York: Spiegel & Grau, 2017).

Davis, A., & West, C. *Freedom Is a Constant Struggle* (red. F. Barat). (Chicago: Haymarket Books, 2016)

Ellemers, Naomi. *Wereld van verschil: Sociale ongelijkheid vanuit een moreel perspectief.* [*A World of Difference: Social Inequality from a Moral Perspective*]. (Amsterdam: Amsterdam University Press, 2017).

Essed, Philomena. *Alledaags racisme.* [*Daily Racism*]. (Amsterdam: Uitgeverij Van Gennep, 2018).

Harari, Yuval Noah. *Sapiens.* (New York: HarperCollins, 2017).

Hermans, Dalilla. *Het laatste wat ik nog wil zeggen over racisme* (red. L. Debacker). [*The Last Thing I Want To Say About Racism*]. (Gent: Borgerhoff & Lamberigts, 2020).

Irving, Debby. *Waking Up White, and Finding Myself in the Story of Race.* (Elephant Room Press, 2014)

Lodik, C. M. *Het antiracismehandboek.* [*The anti-racism handbook*]. (Amsterdam: A.W. Bruna Uitgevers, 2021).

Lorde, Audre. *Sister Outsider: Essays and speeches.* (Trumansburg: Crossing Press, 1984).

Lorde, Audre. *Master's Tools Will Never Dismantle The Master's House* (Penguin Modern Classics Series: 23). (Londen: Penguin Classics, 2021).

Nzume, A., Rouw, E., & El Maslouhi, M. *De goede immigrant* (red. S. Stutgard). [*The Good Immigrant*]. (Amsterdam: Uitgeverij Pluim, 2020).

Nzume, A. *Hallo witte mensen.* [*Hello, White People*]. (Amsterdam: Amsterdam University Press, 2017).

Oluo, I. *So You Want to Talk About Race.* (London: Bloomsbury Publishing, 2019).

Perez, C.C. *Invisible Women: Exposing Data Bias in a World Designed for Men.* (New York: Abrams Books, 2019).

Peter, S. *Coming to Terms with Superdiversity.* (New York: Springer Publishing, 2018).

Repáraz, L.R., Ardjosemito-Jethoe, S., & Rijk, K. *Diversiteit in de samenleving: Concepten, voorbeelden uit de praktijk en methoden voor de hbo-professional* (2de ed.). [*Diversity in Society: Concepts, Real-world Examples and Methods for the College Professional (second edition)*]. (Assen: Koninklijke Van Gorcum, 2020).

Samuel, Mounir. *Handreiking waarden voor een nieuwe taal.* [*Handbook on Values for a New Language*]. (Amsterdam: Code Diversiteit & Inclusie, 2021).

Schinkel, Willem. *Imagined Societies: A Critique of Immigrant Integration in Western Europe* (reprint ed.). (Cambridge: Cambridge University Press, 2019).

Talbot, M. M., & Charlesworth, K. *Sally Heathcote, Suffragette.* (Oregon: Dark Horse Books, 2014).

Trouillot, M.R. *Silencing the Past: The Power and the Production of* History (2e ed.). (Boston: Beacon Press, 2015).

Ven, A. van der, & Abeln, I. *Wit huiswerk. Hoe kun je bijdragen aan de strijd tegen racisme?* [*White homework. How to Contribute to the Fight against Racism*]. (Amsterdam: De Geus, 2020).

Versluis, A., & Uyttenbroek, E. *Exactitudes.* (New York: Macmillan Publishers, 2002).

Wekker, Gloria. *Witte onschuld: Paradoxen van kolonialisme en ras.* [White Innocence: Paradoxes of Colonialism and Race]. (Amsterdam: Amsterdam University Press, 2018).

The organization

Asare, Janice G. *The Pink Elephant: A practical Guide to Creating an Anti-Racist Organization* (red. D. Palmer). (Amsterdam: Reed Business Education, 2020).

Ashikali, T. S., Erradouani, F., & Groeneveld, S. M. *De meerwaarde van diversiteit in de publieke sector. De rol van diversiteitsbeleid, HRM en leiderschap.* [*The Added Value of Diversity in the Public Sector. The Role of Diversity Policy, HRM and Leadership*]. (Rotterdam: Erasmus Universiteit Rotterdam, 2013).

Braun, Danielle. *Patronen: Herkennen en veranderen met antropologische blik.* [*Patterns: Recognizing and Changing with An Anthropological Perspective*]. (Amsterdam: Boom Uitgevers, 2021).

Çankaya, Sinan. *Buiten veiliger dan binnen: in-en uitsluiting van etnische minderheden binnen de politieorganisatie* (Vol. 18). [*Safer Outside Than Inside: Inclusion and Exclusion of Ethnic Minorities within The Police Force*]. (Utrecht: Eburon Uitgeverij BV, 2011).

Çelik, Saniye. *Sturen op verbinden: De business case van diversiteit van publieke organisaties.* [*The Business Case of Diversity of Public Organizations*]. (Leiden: Hogeschool Leiden, 2016).

Challouki, Hanan. *Inclusive Communication* (Kalmthout: Pelckmans Uitgevers, 2021).

Crul, M., Dick, L., Ghorashi, H., & Jr Valenzuela. A. (red.). *Scholarly Engagement and Decolonisation: Views from South Africa, The Netherlands, and the United States* (*On Higher Education Transformation*). (Stellenbosch: African Sun Media, 2020).

Dijkshoorn, Marianne. *Maak je event toegankelijk.* [*Make Your Event Accessible*]. (Utrecht: BigBusinessPublishers, 2018).

Felten, Hanneke. *Dilemma's én tips bij de ontwikkeling van antidiscriminatie methoden*. [*Dilemmas and Tips in Developing Anti-discrimination Methods*]. (Utrecht: Kennisplatform Integratie & Samenleving, 2020).

Felten, Hanneke, Asante, A., Donker, R., Andriessen, I., Noor, S. *Wat werkt in de aanpak van institutioneel racisme? [What Works in Tackling Institutional Racism?*]. (Utrecht: Kennisplatform Integratie en Samenleving, 2021).

Ferdman, B. M. (2014). "The Practice of Inclusion in Diverse Organizations: Toward a Systemic and Inclusive Framework", In B. M. Ferdman & B. R. Deane (Eds.), *Diversity at Work: The Practice of Inclusion*, (2014) p. 3-54.

Jansen, W. S. *Social inclusion in diverse work settings*. (Kurt Lewin Instituut, 2015).

Otten, S., Der Zee, V.K., & Brewer, M. B. *Towards Inclusive Organizations: Determinants of successful diversity management at work (Current Issues in Work and Organizational Psychology)*. (Londen: Taylor & Francis, Psychology Press, 2014).

Page, Scott. *The Diversity Bonus* (red. E. Lewis & N. Cantor). (Princeton: Princeton University Press, 2019).

Papaikonomou, Zoë, & Dijkman, Annebregt. *'Heb je een boze moslim voor mij?' Over inclusieve journalistiek. ["Got an Angry Muslim for me?" A Book about Inclusive Journalism*]. (Amsterdam: Amsterdam University Press, 2018).

Toorn, Jojanneke. van der. "Naar een inclusieve werkvloer: Seksuele oriëntatie en genderidentiteit op het werk" ["Towards an Inclusive Workplace: Sexual Orientation and Gender Identity at Work"], *Gedrag & Organisatie, 32*(3), (2019) p. 162-180.

Waldring, I. E. *The fine art of boundary sensitivity: Second-generation professionals engaging with social boundaries in the workplace*. (Antwerpen: Universiteit van Antwerpen, 2018).

Webster, J. R., Adams, G. A., Maranto, C. L., & Sawyer, K. "Workplace contextual supports for LGBT employees: A review, meta-analysis, and agenda for future research", *Human Resource Management*, 57, (2018) p. 193-210.

The Manager

Armstrong, K. *Twelve Steps to a Compassionate Life*. (Anchor Publishing, 2011).

Atcheson, S. *Demanding More: Why Diversity and Inclusion Don't Happen and What You Can Do About It*. (Londen: Kogan Page, 2021).

Elburg, Astrid. *4xG: De kracht van vernieuwend leiderschap. [The Power of Innovative Leadership*]. (Amsterdam: Elburg Consultancy, 2012).

Ghorashi, Halleh. *Paradoxen van culturele erkenning: Management van diversiteit in nieuw Nederland. [Paradoxes of Cultural Recognition: Managing Diversity in The New Netherlands*]. (Amsterdam: Vrije Universiteit Amsterdam, 2006).

Jaworski, Joseph. *Synchronicity: The Inner Path of Leadership*. Alameda: Berrett-Koehler Publishers, 2000)

Kahane, A. *Power and Love: A Theory and Practice of Social Change.* (New York: Macmillan Publishers, 2010).

Kahneman, Daniel. *Thinking, Fast and Slow.* (New York: Farrar, Straus and Giroux, 2011).

Loo, H., & Beks, J. *Psychologische veiligheid. [Psychological Safety].* (Amsterdam: Boom Lemma, 2020).

Mollema, Esther. *Succes in veelvoud: Diversiteit doe-het-zelf voor leiders die High Performance Teams willen bouwen. [A Multitude of Success: Diversity DIY for Leaders Who Want to Build High Performance Teams].* (Hilversum: Direction Europe, 2015).

Mor Barak, M. E., Lizano, E. L., Kim, A., Duan, L., Rhee, M. K., Hsiao, H. Y., & Brimhall, K. C. "The promise of diversity management for climate of inclusion: A state-of-the-art review and meta-analysis", Human Service Organizations: Management, Leadership & Governance, *40*(4), (2016) p. 305-333.

Smit, P., & Szapora, A. *Veranderen voor luie mensen. [Change for Lazy People].* (Amsterdam: Spectrum, 2020)

Spier, M. *Impact: Lessen in persoonlijk en zakelijk leiderschap. [Impact: Lessons in Personal and Business Leadership].* (Amsterdam: Uitgeverij Pluim, 2021).

Sweeney, C., & Bothwick, F. *Inclusive Leadership: The Definitive Guide to Developing and Executing an Impactful Diversity and Inclusion Strategy.* (London: Pearson Education Limited, 2016).

Syed, J., & Ozbilgin, M. *Managing Diversity and Inclusion.* (Thousand Oaks, Californië: SAGE Publications, 2019).

Williams, J.C., & Dempsey, R. *What Works for Women at Work.* (Amsterdam: Amsterdam University Press, 2018).

The Diversity Practitioner & Knowledge is Power

Ahmed, Sara. *On Being Included: Racism and Diversity in Institutional Life.* (Durham: Duke University Press, 2012).

Asare, Janice G. *Dirty Diversity: A Practical Guide to Foster an Equitable and Inclusive Workplace for All* (red. D. Palmer). (Amsterdam: Reed Business Education, 2020).

Bos, Marten. *Coaching en diversiteit: Een pragmatische kijk op modellen die werken. [Coaching and Diversity: A Pragmatic Look at Models That Work].* (Houten: Bohn Stafleu van Loghum, 2013).

Brink, Marieke. van den. *De zevenkoppige draak van ongelijkheid: Heldinnen en hindernissen in de queeste naar inclusiviteit. Inaugurele rede. [The Seven-headed Dragon of Inequality: Heroines and Obstacles in the Quest for Inclusion. Inaugural address].* (Amsterdam: Amsterdam University Press, 2017).

Cairo, Aminata. *Holding Space: A Storytelling Approach to Trampling Diversity and Inclusion* (ed. L. Rumbley). (Den Haag: Aminata Cairo Consultancy, 2021).

Çankaya, Sanin. *Mijn ontelbare identiteiten*. [*My Countless Identities*]. (Amsterdam: De Bezige Bij, 2020).

Geffen, Grethe van. *Verschil moet er zijn*. [*Difference Must Exist*]. (Amsterdam: Reed Business Education, 2007).

Newkirk, P. *Diversity Inc.* (New York: Bold Type Books, 2019).

Puwar, N. *Space invaders: Race, Gender and Bodies Out of Place*. (Londen: Bloomsbury Publishing, 2004).

Williams, D.A., & Wade-Golden, K.C. *The Chief Diversity Officer*. (Stylus Publishing, 2013).

Author's Biographies

Tengbeh Kamara

Kauthar Bouchallikht (she/her) has published for various media outlets, has extensive civil society experience and is an intersectional climate activist. She became a member of Dutch Parliament for the green political party GroenLinks is 2021.

Zoë Papaikonomou (she/her) is an author, investigative journalist and lecturer. Her work focuses on diversity, equity and inclusion. Not only by researching this field, but also by challenging current structures and norms. In 2018 she published her first book *'Got an angry Muslim for me?' A book about Inclusive Journalism.*

Printed and bound by CPI Group (UK) Ltd, Croydon, CR0 4YY

13/04/2025

14656555-0001